DATE DUE			

THE WEST BANK DATA PROJECT

A SURVEY OF ISRAEL'S POLICIES

MERON BENVENISTI

American Enterprise Institute for Public Policy Research
Washington and London

MERON BENVENISTI served as deputy mayor of Jersualem and chairman of the Planning and Building Commission (1974–1978). He was also administrator of the Old City and East Jerusalem and a city councillor for the municipality. He is the author of *Crusader Castles in Israel* (1965), *The Crusaders in the Holy Land* (1970), *Jerusalem: The Torn City* (1977), and *The Peace of Jerusalem* (1981), as well as many articles in English and Hebrew for periodicals.

Library of Congress Cataloging in Publication Data

Benvenisti, Meron.
  The West Bank Data project.

  (AEI studies ; 398)
  Includes bibliographical references.
  1. West Bank. 2. Israel—Politics and government. 3. Jewish-Arab relations—1967–1973. 4. Jewish-Arab relations—1973-   . I. Title. II. Series.
  DS119.7.B386   1984   956.95   84-2984
  ISBN 0-8447-3545-0
  ISBN 0-8447-3544-2 (pbk.)

AEI Studies 398

1   3   5   7   9   10   8   6   4   2

Printed in the United States of America

Contents

TABLES

MAPS

Foreword

The Middle East plays a central role in U.S. foreign and economic policy, a fact long recognized by the American Enterprise Institute in its studies, televised forums, symposia, and special analyses. These publications indicate the wide range of complex issues on the Middle East that AEI has identified and studied.

This study by Meron Benvenisti is based on empirical data collected about key aspects of life in the West Bank and Gaza and then analyzed in relation to Israeli policies. The result is a detailed and balanced account supported by a wealth of original research and maps. Because of his analytic ability and his government experience, Dr. Benvenisti is uniquely qualified to write this study.

The American Enterprise Institute has been interested in the future of the West Bank and Gaza since the mid-1970s and has explored this topic from the standpoint of both the Arabs residing in these territories and the Israelis who have governed them since 1967. As part of our continuing research on this subject we have published four studies prior to this one: *The West Bank and Gaza: Toward the Making of a Palestinian State,* by Emile A. Nakhleh (1979); *The Camp David Framework for Peace,* by Daniel J. Elazar (1979); *A Palestinian Agenda for the West Bank and Gaza,* edited by Emile A. Nakhleh (1980); and *Judea, Samaria, and Gaza: Views on the Present and the Future,* edited by Daniel J. Elazar (1982). No topic in American Middle East policy is more contentious or more important than the future of the Palestinians, and no topic deserves more careful review by a research institute.

We wish to acknowledge the support of the Ford Foundation and the Rockefeller Foundation, which made this study possible. Overseeing the study on behalf of AEI was resident fellow Judith Kipper, along with Dr. Robert Pranger, director of international programs, and Harold Saunders, resident fellow. The author's preliminary report was first presented at the American Enterprise Institute on October 27, 1982. Subsequently, representatives of the Ford Foundation and the Rockefeller Foundation and other experts joined AEI Middle East specialists for a two-day session in Washington with the author to review his study and to comment on his manuscript.

It is a pleasure to add Dr. Benvenisti's study to our list of publications on the West Bank and Gaza. We believe that *The West Bank Data Project: A Survey of Israel's Policies* will make a significant contribution to the literature available on the status of the West Bank since 1967. Like our other studies on this subject, this work should be seen as a contribution to the competition of ideas that should take place on all important issues—domestic and foreign—confronting the American system of democratic values and constitutional liberties.

AEI holds a unique place in the nation's capital and in the international exchange of ideas. Our programs and publications are designed to foster thoughtful discussion and analysis of important public policy problems facing world and national leaders. Solid nonpartisan research has made AEI preeminent among scholarly institutions. Our continuing objective is to foster the competition of ideas, which is fundamental to a free society; this publication presents another major point of view to be debated and analyzed.

WILLIAM J. BAROODY
President
American Enterprise Institute

Preface

In slightly more than one year, a generation of Israelis and Palestinians who were born after 1967 will come of age. Those young people have known the reality only of Israeli occupation of the West Bank and Gaza; yet they see this reality solely through the prism of their parents' conceptual framework. For the older generation of Israelis and Palestinians, the last 16 years have been but a short phase in the long and bitter strife that began 101 years ago.

The Israeli-Palestinian conflict, like all intense conflicts involving the most cherished values and rights perceived as inalienable, causes the parties to adopt a selective attitude to real facts. Both Israelis and Palestinians receive only messages that reinforce their partisan perceptions, because only these messages seem to them significant. They see all events in terms of national gain or loss and the world as a disharmonious, conflict-laden environment. Each side views its own values as just, true, and absolute and formulates its ideologies and policies to protect these values against the "other side." This adversarial approach is based on the mechanism of coping with reality by avoiding all those elements that contradict their partisan perceptions. When Israelis and Palestinians write about the occupied territories, the reader has the impression that two different places and two distinct physical and human environments are being described.

Under such circumstances the need for an objective, impartial view seems essential, but third-party intervention in the dichotomous environment is problematic. Outsiders tend to assume two basic roles. The first is that of the objective "professional." Such people are rational actors who ignore perceived reality and concentrate on conflicts of objective interests. For them the politics of the conflict are the root of the problem, not its outcome. Because they are oriented to value-maximizing choice, they employ rational criteria and unbiased expertise based on quantifiable data. The second basic role orientation is that of the "resolver." Resolvers perceive themselves as standing above or outside the conflict and therefore as qualified to view it objectively and to suggest sensible policies and compromises. For them there are no zero-sum conflicts, only conflicts perceived as such.

Resolvers accept the perceived reality of the adversaries as the only meaningful reality and believe that it can be altered by persuading the partisans to accept their harmonious world view.

These objective interventions are problematic and usually ineffective because they suffer from an inherent contradiction: they constitute a third-party attempt to penetrate a binary situation. At best such an attempt seems irrelevant to the adversaries; at worst, it becomes part of the conflict—rejected by both sides or identified by one side as aligned with the other and therefore hostile.

The same inherent problems affect the present study. The original research proposal for the West Bank Data Base Project was defined as "the compilation, analysis, and assessment of all relevant information on the West Bank and Gaza that will reflect the realities of these territories." We who are involved with the project have not attempted to carry out an investigation or to provide objective and impartial testimony. Our intention has been to focus on the fast-changing conditions in the territories and, in so doing, to prevent the political discussion and the decision-making process from being overtaken by events.

We have not escaped the fate of other independent researchers. Indeed, even as we have worked, we have developed an instinct that has allowed us to predict what piece of information would be used against whom. Some parties have identified us as aligned with the "other side." We have not, however, been considered irrelevant. The response of third parties, including policy makers and the press, has been very encouraging, and we feel that we have contributed to the general political discussion. The main source of satisfaction has been that the adversaries themselves have not considered our study irrelevant, even among themselves. Almost at the same time that our interim report was circulated unofficially in the Palestine National Council at Algiers (spring 1983), in Israel our findings triggered a heated discussion of the reversibility of the annexation process.

The encouraging response was marred, however, by a growing sense of despair. Our research showed us the great strength of the forces now perpetuating existing conditions in the territories. We learned that the political, juridical, administrative, social, and psychological processes had already assumed a quasi-permanence. There are strong indications that the critical point has passed and that therefore the whole political discussion, which is based on the premise that things are reversible, is irrelevant and has been overtaken by events. The feeling of impending disaster is stronger because all signs point to the conclusion that the situation should be diagnosed as an endemic malaise resistant to comprehensive surgical remedies.

The Israeli-Palestinian conflict has already entered a new and more sinister phase—it has become an internal, ethnic, organic strife between superiors and inferiors. This new phase requires a total reevaluation of all previous conceptions and demands reformulations of policies by all sides and especially by the conflicting parties. The realization that a turning point has been reached will dawn very slowly upon the adversaries, who are firmly entrenched in their stereotypes. We suspect that we are entering a period of painful adjustment to a new reality. This period is best described in the famous lines of Yeats's "The Second Coming":

> The blood-dimmed tide is loosed, and every-
> where
> The ceremony of innocence is drowned;
> The best lack all conviction, while the worst
> Are full of passionate intensity.

We may only hope that this period of confusion will not last and that young people, Israelis and Palestinians, will free themselves from the fossilized perception of their war-weary, insecure parents and mold a new world in a new image.

The West Bank Data Base Project is a collective endeavor. In the course of the last year we have gathered a vast quantity of data and have stored it in a retrieval system. Fourteen individual research projects were completed by various scholars: demography (Eitan Sabatello); agriculture and water (David Kahan); met-

ropolitan links (Annette Hochstein); security; administration (Zvi Barel); industry (Hillel Frisch); economic costs (Shlomo Maoz); law (David Kretzmer); determinants of migration (Stuart Gabriel); censorship; planning (Aron Turner); Jerusalem (Meron Benvenisti); taxation; settlements. Some of the resulting studies will be published separately. Others have been incorporated in the present book.

Many individuals and institutions helped us plan the project and make it an ongoing center for the gathering and analysis of data. Those whom we wish to mention include Michael Weil, Jeffrey Green, Danny Rubinstein, David Richardson, Yehuda Litani, Usamah Halabi, Erela Brilliant-Levi, Vivienne Levi, Yael Minkoff, Elaine Singer, Mical Sela, Avner Halperin, Dori Baron, Avi Shavit, Gideon Toledano, and Amnon Carmon, all in Israel.

Special thanks to my friends in the United States—Judy Crichton, Joseph Low, Larry Fabian, and Ian Lustick—for constant encouragement and support. My deep gratitude to Judy Barsalou, Gary Sick, and John Stremlau, who not only recognized the importance of the project but also gave of their time to review it in its preliminary stages.

The American Enterprise Institute in Washington, D.C., has been my home away from Jerusalem. I wish to express special thanks to Judith Kipper, Robert Pranger, and Harold Saunders, who assisted me in every possible way. The project is theirs as much as mine. I am deeply indebted to the Rockefeller Foundation and the Ford Foundation for research grants that made the project possible and to the American Jewish Committee for support in the development stages of this project.

Finally, I am grateful to Robert Silvers, editor of *The New York Review of Books*, for permission to use an adaptation of my article, "The Turning Point in Israel," October 13, 1983, as chapter 7 in this volume.

MERON BENVENISTI
Jerusalem

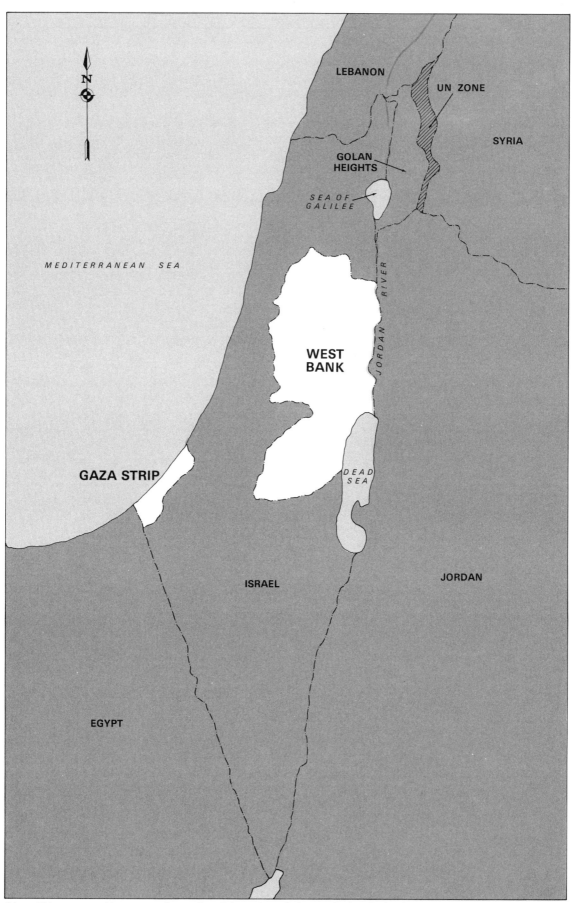

NOTE: This map provides a general overview; it is not intended to imply that the borders are internationally recognized.

1

The Missing Age Group: Demography

The Population Size

Sources of Estimates. The size of the Palestinian population in the West Bank and Gaza can only be estimated. Since 1967 no census has been carried out there, although two have been conducted in Israel, in 1972 and 1983. The available data on population are derived from the current population estimates (CPE) of the Central Bureau of Statistics (CBS) and, separately, from the Ministry of the Interior population register count (PRC). The staff officer in charge of statistics in the military government (MG) from time to time publishes his own estimates in the military government's annual reports. The three estimates are based on different methods and therefore differ considerably. Although the CPE for the West Bank population at the end of 1980 was 704,000 persons, the PRC estimated the population at 887,000 and the MG at 750,000.

CBS sources criticize PRC estimates as being grossly inflated, mainly because death registration has been faulty. Underreporting of deaths is a well-known phenomenon. It not only causes higher population estimates but also distorts age structure and dependency rate. Demographic estimates based on the PRC conflict with almost all other available demographic information and therefore will not be used in this study. It should be noted, however, that CBS estimates are also based on mortality model tables that are constantly being revised. Recent revisions place the estimated population size 3 percent higher than the figure previously quoted.

East Jerusalem. Since September 1967, population tables for the West Bank have excluded the Palestinian population of East Jerusalem. This omission affects not only the total population but also the annual growth rate, because East Jerusalem and the rest of the West Bank have different growth rates. The average population growth rate in East Jerusalem for 1967–1980 was estimated at 3.0 percent per annum, compared with 1.4–1.5 percent in the West Bank. In May 1967 there were 80,000 inhabitants in East Jerusalem, in September 1967 there were 67,000, and at the end of 1982 there were 120,000 (14 percent of the combined population of East Jerusalem and the West Bank).

The West Bank and Gaza. Table 1 shows the development of the population in the West Bank and Gaza. One striking phenomenon is the almost identical absolute increase of the populations in the West Bank and Gaza between 1922 and 1982—about half a million persons. In 1946 the population in the Gaza region amounted to 15 percent of the West Bank population. In 1982 the Gaza population rose to 55 percent of the West Bank population (including East Jerusalem). This dramatic redistribution of the Palestinian population was caused mainly by the inflow of 165,000 refugees to the Gaza Strip in 1948–1949 but also by different migration patterns in the two regions after the 1948 war (I shall shortly describe the patterns).

Growth Rates. The average annual growth rates of the Arab populations in the two regions are summarized in table 2 together with the growth rate of a third group, the Palestinians under Israeli control, that is, the Israeli Arab group. The differences between the growth rates are easy to recognize. The Israeli Arab population enjoyed very high growth, caused by high fertility, low mortality, and no emigration. The unusually high growth rates in the Israeli Arab sector began to decline in the 1970s because of improved socioeconomic and educational conditions.

The Gaza Strip growth rate shows a remarkably steady pattern. By contrast, the growth rate of the West Bank population fluctuates, mainly because of unequal out-migration waves. For the three Palestinian groups under Israeli control combined, population growth between 1970 and 1980 reached 2.9 percent per annum.

1

TABLE 1

DEVELOPMENT OF THE POPULATION IN THE WEST BANK AND THE GAZA STRIP, 1922–1982

	West Bank		Gaza Strip	
Year	Population (thousands)[a]	Average growth rate per year (percent)	Population (thousands)	Average growth rate per year (percent)
1922	257.5		28.8	
		2.5		5.8
1931	322.2		48.0	
		2.5		2.7
1946	465.8		71.0	
		10.0		(25.0)
1952	742.3		268.0[b]	
		0.9		(2.5)
1961	805.4		—	
		0.9		—
May 1967	845.0		385.0[c]	
		—		—
Sept. 1967	595.9		389.7	
		1.4		−0.7
1970	607.8		370.0	
		2.2		3.0
1975	675.2		425.5	
		1.5		1.4[d]
1980	724.3		456.5	
		1.6		2.2
1982	747.5		476.3	

NOTE: Figures for 1922, 1931, 1952, 1961, and September 1967 are census data; those for all other dates (except May 1967) are end-of-year figures.
a. Figures do not include East Jerusalem after May 1967, when its population was approximately 80,000; in September 1967 its inhabitants numbered 67,000 and by the end of 1982 about 120,000.
b. End-of-year gross estimate based on the assumption of an annual growth rate of 3 percent between 1946 and 1952 and an inflow of 164,000 refugees from the Israeli area during the 1948–1949 war.
c. Gross estimate based on the assumption of an average annual growth rate of 2.5 percent.
d. Not including East Jerusalem.
SOURCE: Eitan Sabatello, "The Population of the Administered Territories," West Bank Data Base Project, July 1983 (draft), table 1.

TABLE 2

AVERAGE ANNUAL GROWTH RATES OF THE ARAB POPULATIONS IN THE AREAS OF THE FORMER MANDATORY PALESTINE, 1922–1981
(per 1,000 population)

Years	Gaza Strip	West Bank	Israel
1922–1947	3.8		2.5[a]
1952–1961	3.0[b]	0.9	3.5
1961–1967	2.5[b]	0.9	4.6
1969–1974	2.7[b]	2.4[b]	4.4
1975–1979	2.8[b,c]	1.5[b]	3.7
1980–1981	2.7[b]	0.8[b]	3.1

NOTE: Growth rates during the periods following a war (and major displacements) are not included.
a. Combined growth of the West Bank and Israel.
b. Approximate rate.
c. Not including the return of El Arish population to Egypt in 1979.
SOURCE: Sabatello, "Population," table 2.

The growth rate of the Jewish population in the same period nearly equaled the combined Arab growth, reaching 2.7 percent per annum. This growth rate was caused by natural increase of 1.5 percent and net immigration of 1.2 percent. Consequently the ratio between Jews and Arabs in Palestine (Israel and the occupied territories) remained constant, the Jewish population constituting roughly 65 percent and the Arab population 35 percent.

Fertility and Mortality

Fertility Levels and Their Socioeconomic Effects. The fertility level of the West Bank population has remained unchanged in the last five decades. The crude birthrate remained about forty-five per thousand, the absolute number of births in the 1970s was about 30,000 a year, and the fertility rate was 7 children per woman. Fertility in Gaza is higher because of a more favorable age-sex population structure (out-migration from the West Bank affected sex structure; see the section "Out-Migration"), reaching fifty per thousand; the number of births per annum has been 20,000; and the fertility rate was 7.2 children per woman in 1980. Higher fertility rates in Gaza are attributed to the greater accessibility of health services provided by the United Nations Relief and Works Agency (UNRWA) and by other organizations.

The fertility pattern both in the West Bank and in Gaza may well have been influenced by education and by improved socioeconomic conditions. In this connection we should notice the dramatic increase in secondary education among women. Of the West Bank women who were born in about 1960, 57 percent have attained postelementary education, compared with 20 percent who were born in about 1950. The change in Gaza has been less dramatic. There 45 percent of the women born in 1960 and 43 percent of the women born in 1950 have attained postelementary education.

The following data indicate improvements in housing conditions: during the 1970s dwelling density decreased; the number of houses supplied with running water doubled (in Gaza it quadrupled); and the share of households supplied with electricity rose from 23 percent in 1967 to 51 percent in the West Bank and from 18 percent to 89 percent in Gaza. The motorization rate (number of cars per 1,000 persons) tripled (see also the section "Individual Prosperity").

Life Expectancy. Underregistration of deaths, especially among the newborn and the elderly, has been a problem for population experts since the British Mandate. As a result life expectancy and especially infant mortality estimates have caused considerable controversy among demographers. Life expectancy among the Palestinian Arab population was estimated in 1947 at about forty-six years. Infant mortality in 1966 was estimated at 15 percent. CBS estimated that the infant mortality rate (IMR) in the West Bank dropped to 10 percent in the mid-1970s. This figure is higher than the registered IMR, which was recorded at 8.6 percent in 1969–1972 and 4.3 percent in 1974–1975. The lower figures, however, are clearly defective. CBS assesses the infant mortality rate for the early 1980s at 7 percent for both Gaza and the West Bank. The estimated life expectancy is estimated at slightly more than sixty years.

Health Conditions. Decreased mortality is reflected in health data. Access to health services has increased. Admission to hospitals and to outpatient clinics rose considerably, death associated with hospitalization decreased, and vaccination of newborns became routine. The percentage of births occurring in hospitals doubled (from 20 percent to 40 percent),

although it is still less than half the percentage prevailing among Israeli Arabs. The improved standard of living and education would contribute to decreased mortality and longer life expectancy.

Out-Migration

Historical Overview. The single most important factor affecting demographic trends in the West Bank is migration. During the mandate period net positive migration from the neighboring countries to Palestine remained relatively high. Even then, however, the area that became known as the West Bank experienced out-migration from the hilly area to the coastal towns, especially to Jaffa and Haifa.

During 1948–1949, 250,000 refugees left the area controlled by Israel and entered the West Bank. The refugees who entered the Gaza Strip numbered 160,000.

The Jordanian Period. The net negative migration during Jordanian rule was very high. It reached an estimated 2.5 percent average per annum and almost offset the natural increase. The number of West Bankers who emigrated between 1948 and 1967 is estimated at almost 400,000 persons. During the period between the two Jordanian censuses (1952 and 1961), the population of the West Bank increased by a mere 63,000, or 0.9 percent per annum. Most migrants moved to the East Bank. Between 1951 and 1962 the relative population weight of the West Bank compared with Transjordan changed from 51.5 percent to 42.7 percent. Jordanian policies of accelerated industrial and agricultural development on the East Bank as well as political and administrative measures created a strong immigration pull, especially to the Amman-Zarqa area.

Palestinian out-migration went beyond the East Bank. Although the exact numbers are unknown, the size of the dispersal of Palestinians is indicated by the 1961 Jordanian census. Of all Jordanian citizens (East and West Bank) who reported one member of the family staying abroad, three-quarters were West Bank Palestinians. The out-migration was selective in age and sex. During the 1950s the majority of emigrants were males under forty. During the 1960s there was a trend toward family reunions, and the rate at which women and children emigrated increased considerably. This trend accelerated between June and September 1967. The propensity to emigrate from the West Bank during the Jordanian period was not uniform. The Christian emigration rate was higher than the Moslem, and refugee camp dwellers were less likely to emigrate than permanent inhabitants. The highest rate was found among refugees living outside camps.

The West Bank and Gaza. Out-migration has less importance in the demographic pattern of the Gaza Strip than in the West Bank. During the 1950s the Egyptian authorities restricted population movement but in the 1960s out-migration increased, although it remained much lower than in the West Bank. In Gaza, as in the West Bank, emigration was much higher among town dwellers than among the refugees living in camps.

As a direct result of the 1967 war, not less than one-fifth of the West Bank population crossed the Jordan. Between June and September 1967, 200,000 left; 15,000 did so during 1968. During 1967–1968, 31,000, or about 8 percent, of the Gaza Strip population emigrated. More than half the emigrants were women and young children.

The out-migration balance of the West Bank and Gaza appears in table 3. During 1969–1974, the West

Bank experienced the lowest migration rate in two decades, for reasons that I shall discuss shortly. Since 1975, however, migration rates have reached the pre-1967 level, though remaining below the 2.5 percent rate prevailing under Jordan. Since 1968, 136,500 Palestinians have left the West Bank, and 90,000 have left Gaza. These figures equal 46 percent and 49 percent of the natural increase in the two regions, respectively. During 1980–1981 almost three-quarters of the natural increase was countered by emigration. Gaza out-migration has remained steady at less than half the West Bank rate.

Consequently, the growth rate in the West Bank (net natural increase less out-migration) during the Israeli occupation has been on the average about 1.5 percent (compared with 0.9 percent during the Jordanian period) and in Gaza about 2.3 percent. The accelerated rate of migration between 1979 and 1981 showed signs of slowing down in 1982–1983 because of the new regulations imposed by Jordan on immigration flow from the West Bank and because of worsening economic and employment conditions in the Arab oil-producing countries.

Emigrant Characteristics. The propensity to migrate has correlated with various characteristics. Emigration has been particularly high among men in their teens and twenties. The emigration rates of women are lower in general; however, there are indications that middle-aged women and their children emigrate to join their husbands. The propensity to emigrate is apparently higher among Palestinians with secondary or postsecondary education. The brain drain can be illustrated by statistics provided by the Kuwait census of 1975, which shows that 44 percent of the employed "Jordanians" and Palestinians were in the professions and in administrative jobs.

The Brain Drain. In the early 1980s the West Bank educational system produced about 9,000 high school graduates and 1,500 postsecondary graduates a year. About 1,000 West Bank students graduate from universities abroad. It is estimated that half of them are seeking employment. The total number of positions attractive to high school graduates in the West Bank does not exceed 14,000, a ratio of three positions for every job seeker (the ratio is 14:1 in Israel). The actual job vacancies are very few, estimated at approximately 1,000. The low number of white-collar vacancies is caused by the very low recruitment rate in the military government (about 300 a year), stagnation in the financial and managerial sectors of the West Bank economy, and the fact that Israeli economy is open only to blue-collar workers. Consequently only 20 percent of high school and university graduates can find employment in any given year, and they either seek em-

TABLE 3

NET MIGRATION BALANCE IN THE WEST BANK AND THE GAZA STRIP, 1967–1981

Year	West Bank		Gaza Strip	
	No.	No. per 1,000	No.	No. per 1,000
1967 (Sept.–Dec.)	– 13,000	– 21.8	– 12,300	– 33.5
1968	– 15,700	– 25.6	– 32,400	– 85.1
Total, 1967–1968	– 28,700	—	– 44,700	—
1969	1,200	2.1	– 2,900	– 8.1
1970	– 5,000	– 8.3	– 3,300	– 9.0
1971	– 2,500	– 4.1	– 2,400	– 6.5
1972	– 5,100	– 8.2	– 3,900	– 10.3
1973	300	0.5	1,700	– 4.4
1974	– 2,700	– 4.1	– 1,900	– 4.7
Total, 1969–1974	– 13,800	—	– 12,700	—
1975	– 15,100	– 22.5	– 3,800	– 9.2
1976	– 14,500	– 21.4	– 4,300	– 10.1
1977	– 10,400	– 15.2	– 3,000	– 6.9
1978	– 9,400	– 13.5	– 5,200	– 11.5
1979	– 11,700	– 16.5	– 4,800	– 10.4
Total, 1975–1979	– 61,100	—	– 21,100	—
1980	– 17,100	– 23.7	– 5,100	– 11.5
1981	– 15,800	– 21.7	– 5,400	– 11.8
Total, 1980–1981	– 32,900	—	– 10,500	—

SOURCE: Sabatello, "Population," table 10.

ployment abroad or work as blue-collar laborers.

The devastating effect of the continued drain of West Bankers in their prime can be illustrated by the following figures: of West Bankers who were between the ages of ten and twenty-four years in 1961 (thirty to forty-four in 1981), only 27 percent of the men and 40 percent of the women have remained in the country. Of the total initial cohort aged ten to twenty-one in 1967 (twenty-four to thirty-five in 1981), only 30 percent of the men and 50 percent of the women continue to live in the West Bank.

Determinants of Migration

Political Overtones. Migration from the West Bank and Gaza is viewed with particular concern in light of its decisive effect on the "demographic balance" in the territories, which is considered a highly political issue. Because of its political implications, emigration is analyzed in relation to political forces, and most analysts intuitively stress Israeli policies of control as the prime cause for Palestinian emigration. Although policies of control and the general political environment undoubtedly play an important role in the propensity to emigrate, it seems that the causes are more complex. The political forces influence migration not directly but rather through economic policies and economic variables.

Economic Variables. Results of an econometric analysis of the determinants of migration from the West Bank and Gaza indicate the relevance of traditional economic variables in an explanation of the controversial migratory phenomenon. The variables used are percentage of change in real per capita consumption/expenditure (in the territories); construction starts expressed in square meters (in the territories as an indication of economic and housing conditions); unilateral transfers to the administered territories; new Israeli settlements; the unemployment rate in the United States (as an indication of economic opportunities in the Western world); and the unemployment rate in Israel. All regression coefficients show that economic development and improved housing diminish the rate of Palestinian out-migration. The same effect is detected for an increase in private unilateral transfers and diminished unemployment in the United States. The emigration rate increases with the rise of the Israeli unemployment rate.

Symbiotic Development. There is also an indication, though tentative, that the building of Israeli settlements tends to diminish the rate of emigration. This finding seems paradoxical, because the settlements arouse political insecurity, increase friction, and cause

hardships that may result in increased migration. The building of settlements, however, almost exclusively carried out by Palestinian manpower, also creates favorable economic conditions. This tentative finding is sustained by study of the differential migratory pattern of growth rates in the Jerusalem metropolitan area, as we shall see. It also indicates the symbiotic economic development of the Jewish and Arab sectors, which is a well-known phenomenon in the economic history of Palestine. The analysis also suggests that the PLO-Jordanian funding of *sumud* (steadfastness) is a factor contributing to diminished out-migration, as is consistent with the political aims of that funding. Paradoxically, the Israeli "creation of physical facts" by taking possession of land and building settlements in the territories, intended to increase the ratio of the Jewish population, has the opposite effect of diminishing migration and increasing Palestinian population growth.

Internal Migration

Limitations of the Data. Data on internal migration in the West Bank are scanty and unreliable because they are based on the Ministry of Interior's PRC, as previously noted. There are indications, however, of a higher growth rate in the southern West Bank than in the northern subdistricts and a higher growth rate in West Bank cities than in the countryside. According to the PRC, the population growth per annum of Ramallah (1961–1981) reached 5.3 percent and that of Nablus 6 percent. Available data suggest that the process of urbanization has accelerated in the West Bank (see chapter 3 and the section "Built-up Areas").

East Jerusalem. The population growth of East Jerusalem has been constant at about 3 percent per annum, higher than the Jewish rate, thus mildly changing the demographic composition of the city. The Jewish majority has decreased by 3–4 percent in sixteen years. There are no reliable figures on population growth in the metropolitan area of Jerusalem outside the city's municipal boundaries, but estimates indicate a similar growth rate of 3 percent in the area surrounding the city. In 1969, 37 percent of the total population of the West Bank southern districts resided in the Jerusalem metropolitan area. In 1980 the figure exceeded 50 percent.

Population Forecasts

The West Bank and Gaza. Official population forecasts assume a more or less constant ratio of natural increase in the West Bank and in Gaza. The rate (predicting a mild decrease in fertility and mortality) is about 3 percent per annum and almost 4 percent in Gaza. If the high emigration rate experienced between 1975 and 1981 is sustained, the population growth rate in the West Bank in the 1980s is predicted to be 1 percent per annum and about 2.5 percent per annum in Gaza. If emigration ceases, however, the growth rates for the West Bank will reach 3 percent and close to 4 percent for Gaza. (These estimates do not take into account a recurrence of catastrophic periods.) The absolute figures for the two regions will therefore be 815,000 (low alternative) to 1 million (high alternative) by 1991 in the West Bank and 600,000–650,000 in Gaza. We should add about 146,000 East Jerusalem residents to the figures for the West Bank.

The Jewish-Arab Ratio. If we assume a constant Jewish growth rate of about 2.5 percent (1.5 percent natural increase and 1 percent net Jewish immigration), as in the 1970s and a 3.2 percent growth rate of the Israeli Arab population, the demographic ratio of roughly two-thirds Jews and one-third Arabs in Western Palestine will be maintained in 1991. The so-called demographic threat, that is, the gradually increasing proportion of Arabs versus Jews, a notion that is widespread in Israeli dovish political thinking, is not upheld by the data.

The Effects of Normal and Catastrophic Conditions. Demographic trends in the West Bank and Gaza were shaped mainly by the rate of migration. We have witnessed two distinct periods in the last thirty-five years: normal periods and catastrophic periods. Normal periods are characterized by emigration caused by pushes and pulls, that is, by the relative effects of economic, legal, and political conditions in the sending and receiving areas. In normal conditions the emigration wave initially consists of men in their prime, followed later by middle-aged women and their children. The extent of emigration during normal times is difficult to predict because the pushes and pulls are independent variables. An increase in the Israeli unemployment rate tends to increase emigration considerably. Economic difficulties in the Arab Gulf states tend to decrease emigration. Administrative restrictions on long-term stay in the receiving countries diminish emigration, but political harassment in the sending area may strengthen the propensity to emigrate.

Catastrophic periods are characterized by mass emigration in short periods of time, when whole families, with a high ratio of nonworking people (elderly, children, middle-aged women) to workers, move abroad. These waves are associated with hostilities or wars and last a few months after the cessation of hostilities.

The occurrence of catastrophic periods in a volatile area like the Middle East is very hard to predict, and therefore all reasonable forecasts of population size and rate of growth must assume normal conditions. These are influenced by political, economic, social, and psychological variables that are very difficult to weigh. As a result all emigration projections seem highly speculative.

Conclusion

One unequivocal conclusion can be drawn from the survey of demographic trends in the West Bank and Gaza. The Palestinian population has been totally at the mercy of outside forces that have affected its size by controlling migration rates. The Jordanians have created and maintained political and economic pulls that induced the highest emigration rate to date; the Egyptians restricted emigration from Gaza and therefore induced a very high rate of population growth in the area; the Israelis opened the domestic labor market to unskilled Palestinian workers and therefore caused the lowest rate of emigration in a generation. When, after 1974, the Israeli economic development slowed down, emigration rates soared. The "open bridges" created a quasi-normal push-and-pull condition, and the rate of Palestinian migration was subjected to the political, administrative, and economic decisions of both Israel and Jordan, sometimes working in tandem and sometimes conflicting.

Palestinian migration is almost totally dependent on outside forces, and there are no economic, political, or psychological forces within the territories that can influence migratory trends. This dependence is but one manifestation of the Palestinians' inability to influence their future. The same subservient role of the Palestinians is manifest in the internal migratory pattern. The single most important factor determining internal migration in the West Bank is Israeli development of settlements, which leads Arabs to commute to construction sites.

If existing processes continue, we should expect an accelerated gravitation of Palestinians to the metropolitan area of Jerusalem. The rate of urbanization would increase, and depopulation of relatively remote villages would continue. The emphasis on settlement in Western Samaria will create a semiurban region east of the Green Line, which will comprise the semiurban Israeli Arab region extending from Taybah to Baqa al-Gharbiyya and the triangle Tul Karm-Qalqiliya-Salfit. Israeli planners consider Palestinian urbanization unfavorable because it tends to create political centers of gravity and to move peasants from their traditional environment into a new and more hostile political environment. Therefore policies of containment are suggested, especially checks on the development of Arab towns and the encouragement of village development. It remains to be seen whether these policies will be successful. Still, the ability of the Palestinian community to plan its own population dispersal is, at any rate, very limited.

Notes

The data in this chapter are based on E. Sabatello, *The Populations of the Administered Territories: Some Demographic Trends and Implications* (Jerusalem: West Bank Data Base Project, forthcoming), and S. Gabriel, *The Determinants of Labor Migration from the West Bank and Gaza* (Jerusalem: West Bank Data Base Project, forthcoming).

2
Prosperity and Stagnation: The Economy

Overview

National Accounting. The occupied territories are treated in the professional (and political) literature as a distinct economic entity within defined geographic boundaries (the Green Line). Economic activity in the territories is monitored just as it is in any national economy. The territories have their separate national accounts: gross domestic product (GDP), gross national product (GNP), balance-of-payments, and resources and uses tables are published annually. Israeli economists view the economic interaction of Israel and the territories as a common market. Palestinian economists define the relationship as imperial-colonial interaction. The economic data do not easily fit either definition. The patterns of economic growth seem to economists unusual or idiosyncratic. Some conflicting trends include a large gap between GDP and GNP; minimal production generating capital investment; diminishing expenditure on general public consumption; dramatic growth in per capita GNP; a high and diminishing ratio of private consumption; investment in housing that accounts for more than half of the growing private investment; relatively minor changes in the weight of economic branches; the rapid growth of GDP; the continued predominance of primary branches (agriculture, quarrying); and the stagnation of industry. The West Bank and Gaza are protected outlets for Israeli manufactured goods and a cheap source for unskilled labor and therefore fit classic colonial patterns. At the same time, there has been no worsening of the terms of trade or change in the resource base that existed before the occupation; diversification has been handicapped by the restriction of exports to the Arab market, and productivity has increased mainly through implementation of modern technologies.

Regional Economy. It seems that the contradictory patterns of economic growth can be partly explained by abandoning the national economy model and analyzing the economy of the West Bank and Gaza as it has always been—a fragmented and undeveloped regional economy with boundaries arbitrarily defined by military and political circumstances; it has never been allowed to develop as an independent economic unit or even to forge meaningful interactions among its diverse branches.

The territories, we should recall, constituted less than a quarter of Mandatory Palestine's land mass and contributed no more than 10 percent to its GDP. The development of the Palestinian economy was concentrated in the coastal plain, and although the hilly area benefited from the spillover of economic boom in the 1940s, it remained basically a stagnant region of subsistence agriculture. The four subregions—Nablus, Jerusalem, Hebron, and Gaza—never maintained strong economic ties.

The hilly areas were lumped together into the West Bank as a result of the 1948 war, and Gaza became a dead-end appendage of the Sinai desert. Before they could develop any degree of interaction the hilly areas were forcefully integrated into a new economic system, that of the East Bank. The economic policies of the Hashemites perpetuated the fragmented nature of the West Bank economy and established its growth pattern: labor intensive, with primary economic branches (agriculture and quarrying), a low level of industrialization, a migratory labor force, a substantial gap between GNP and GDP, minimal investment in infrastructure, and a low level of government expenditure. Administrative measures enforced subregional segmentation and the transfer of private initiative and investment to the East Bank.

Conditions under Jordan. The result of the economic policies was that the East Bank developed rapidly at the expense of the West Bank. In 1967 the value added of the industrial sector in the East Bank was almost triple that of the West Bank, whereas in 1948 the reverse had been true. In the early 1950s the GDP of the West Bank was considerably higher than that of the East Bank. In 1967 GDP was one-third higher in the East Bank and per capita GNP 50 percent higher than in the West Bank. Although industrial development was minimal (only ten large industrial plants were established), the West Bank provided Jordan with 50 percent of its vegetables, 40 percent of its livestock and dairy products, and all of its olive and olive oil produce. It also provided the East Bank with the manpower (unskilled, skilled, and managerial) necessary for the development of the desert kingdom. Viewed as an independent economic entity, the West Bank under Jordan can be defined as nonviable and unbalanced. It had never, however, been the intention of Jordanian economic decision makers to allow the formation of a Palestinian economic entity. The West Bank economy had its assigned role as a subservient sector within the framework of the Jordanian economy. Such is the power of sovereign states operating from self-interest.

Little can be said about the economy of the Gaza Strip. The Egyptians simply ignored this impoverished territory, swamped by refugees from southern Palestine and lacking any economic viability except for citrus groves and fishing. We need mention only that in 1966 per capita GNP in Gaza, at eighty dollars, was one of the lowest in the world.

Conditions under Israel. The 1967 war disrupted the economic system of the West Bank for the second time in a generation. This time the consequences of the geopolitical upheaval were even more dramatic than they had been after 1948. The West Bank economy was confronted with an economic giant. The total GNP of the West Bank and Gaza combined amounted to 2.6 percent of Israel's GNP. By 1980, after thirteen years of rapid growth, it reached 5.2 percent of Israel's GNP. Israel's export alone exceeded the GNP of both territories. Per capita GNP in Israel was, in 1965, six times the per capita GNP of the West Bank (in 1980 it was 3.5 times greater). The value added of the industrial sector of the West Bank and Gaza is 1 percent of Israel's industrial sector. Even in agriculture, which contributes almost 30 percent to the West Bank GNP, the value of production amounts to 29 percent of Israeli agriculture, which contributes a mere 5.5 percent to its GNP. The total purchasing power of more than a million Palestinians and Gazans amounts (after a dramatic increase in per capita income of 10 percent per annum for fifteen years) to the purchasing power of a middle-sized Israeli city.

The Israeli occupation did not create the territories' economic malaise. It only aggravated it. The fragmented, nonviable, dependent, underdeveloped nature of its economic branches became more visible as a result of the tremendous disparity between them and the Israeli economic sectors. Instead of being sub-

servient and auxiliary to the less-developed Jordanian economy, the territories were sucked into the highly developed Israeli system. The outcome was inevitable: the economy of the West Bank and Gaza was fully integrated within that of Israel. The local, daily interaction across invisible boundaries, subcontracting, the commuting of tens of thousands of workers, and the building of Jewish industrial estates in the West Bank rendered the term "territories' economic entity" as appropriate as the term "Beersheeba economic entity."

Individual Prosperity. Economic integration has been beneficial to the territories' inhabitants individually. The gap between their disposable income and that of Israelis has narrowed by almost 50 percent. Although in 1967 they lagged behind the East Bank, in 1980 their average income equaled that of Jordan. The nutritional value of their food is the highest among the Arab countries. In 1972, 35 percent of the households were connected to the electric grid, and 14 percent possessed refrigerators. In 1981 the figures were 80 percent and 51 percent, respectively. The rate of motorization tripled in ten years, and illiteracy diminished from 48 percent in 1970 to 29 percent in 1980. Some economic branches have also prospered. Integration into the Israeli economy, however, dealt a death blow to the economic viability of the Palestinians as a community.

Benefits without Burdens. The Israelis have kept up the facade of the territories' separate economic entity. Paradoxically, under Israeli rule the Palestinians were granted, for the first time in their economic history, the status of a national economy. Separate national accounts, separate economic policies, and separate administrative arrangements have been maintained by the Israelis while at the same time total integration has been enforced. The reason is obvious: the Israelis wanted the benefits of integration without its burdens. Formal integration would have meant extending the social welfare state system that dominates the economic scene in Israel. This system is characterized by selective taxation and massive subsidies, direct involvement in refinancing, infrastructure development, massive aid in recession periods, differential tariffs, and foreign currency manipulations. Treating the territories as "a quasi-national economy in common market with Israel" enabled the Israelis to avoid such burdens and to protect their own economy from potential competition.

1967–1973. To be sure, economic policies followed evolving political perceptions. After the 1967 war Israeli leaders perceived the occupation as temporary and believed that within a framework of "territorial compromises" the territories would be returned to Jordan but would maintain a common market with Israel (or at least "open frontiers"). Worried about the political and social burdens of "changing the nature of the Jewish state" by absorbing the "heavily populated regions," Israeli politicians were also concerned about the economic burdens of integrating the Palestinian economy; hence the rigid separation of the two economies during the first years of occupation and the initiation of an elaborate system of bookkeeping and licensing. The first years of occupation were also the "self-conscious" years of Israeli administration, a period in which Israel saw itself as a quasi-trustee of the territories, responsible for their political and economic progress. Just as the Israelis initiated local elections and the enfranchisement of women, they embarked upon large-scale development projects in agriculture and, to some extent, in industry.

1973–1975. The optimistic, solution-oriented mood vanished in the aftermath of the 1973 war. The hopes for a political solution faded, and the economic burdens of the occupation were found to be surprisingly light. The "separate economic entity," as a provisional arrangement, was found to be a convenient device for accruing substantial benefits with negligible costs.

Gastarbeiter. The Israeli economy was ready to use its own *Gastarbeiter.* Jewish laborers who were laid off in the construction sector during a recession in 1966 did not go back to manual labor. Their place was taken by laborers from the territories who very quickly amounted to almost one-third of the total labor force in the construction branch and constituted a majority of unskilled laborers on actual construction sites. The significance of the Palestinian labor force is marginal in the Israeli labor market (3.5–5 percent of the total labor force, more than 8 percent of the work force in production). In labor-intensive, low-wage, and low-prestige sectors, however, the Palestinians' effect is significant. They are heavily concentrated in municipal sanitation, in menial hospital and hotel jobs, and in gardening, and often work as gas station employees and as restaurant dishwashers. The supply of cheap labor had important economic benefits. It mitigated the pressures for higher wages and therefore contributed to faster economic growth and lower inflation rates. The supply of unskilled workers enabled labor-intensive branches to prosper. It also delayed, and even eliminated, the need for capital investment in mechanization.

Imports and Exports. The territories became in addition an important outlet for manufactured goods. In the peak year (1975) 16 percent of total Israeli exports were sold in the territories. In later years the percent-

age decreased to 10.4 percent (1980); but the West Bank has remained a larger market for Israeli goods than Britain and Germany and amounted to 60 percent of the size of the U.S. market. It has been a protected market. High tariffs and rigid policies of import licensing ensured marketing of high-priced and low-quality Israeli products.

The territories' "exports" to Israel consist mainly of goods manufactured under subcontracting arrangements with Israeli firms producing food, textiles, leather, and building material. The total export to Israel amounts to 20 percent of the GDP of the territories. The sale of agricultural products has been restricted to prevent competition with Israeli farmers.

There has been a constant net deficit in the balance of trade between Israel and the territories. The deficit has been covered mainly by wages earned by laborers in Israel but also by foreign currency transfers from Jordan, either private (laborers abroad) or institutional (Jordanian–Palestine Liberation Organization [PLO], UNRWA, voluntary agencies). To Israel the territories have been a net foreign currency earner.

Budgets. An analysis of government budgets shows how light the fiscal burden has been. Two-thirds of military government expenditure on the local population has been covered by revenues collected from the population. Development budgets have been minimal. There has been no monetary burden, since there are no Israeli credit facilities on the West Bank and the other monetary arrangements (such as dual currency and currency controls) are beneficial to Israel. There are indications that the territories place no fiscal and monetary burden on Israel. In fact, if we calculate total Israeli government expenditure (including social security to laborers) against total revenues (including income tax on laborers and customs), it may well be that the territories are a net source of revenue to the Israeli Treasury.

From an economic point of view there is no need to get rid of the territories. On the contrary, a separate economic entity controlled by Israel offers great economic advantages.

Integration and Segregation. An interim political-economic policy to keep options open (or "to decide not to decide") became a long-term policy—to integrate while unequally segregating. The "national accounting," published dutifully every year, became a useful and respectable device for granting legitimacy to institutional discrimination. It was the economic embodiment of the Israeli concept of "military occupation," legitimizing a dual legal and administrative system.

In the late 1970s, the territories' "separate economic entity" lost even its imaginary territorial base.

The economic activity of the Israeli settlers in the West Bank and Gaza, the production of their industrial estates, and their consumption patterns are recorded in the national accounts of Israel, and rightly so. After all, they belong to the Israeli welfare state and operate within its legal, administrative, and economic system. The Central Bureau of Statistics still labels its reports "national accounts for Judea, Samaria, and the Gaza Strip." In fact, however, these accounts include data concerning the economic situation only of the local population, those people who are fully integrated individually but are effectively excluded communally.

The ethnic economic data provided by the national accounts illustrate clearly the disparity between individual prosperity and communal stagnation. Individual prosperity is based mainly on the purchasing power of laborers in Israel, which amounts to one-third of the total resources of the territories. Communal stagnation is caused by discriminatory terms of trade, lack of protection, credit, infrastructure, or subsidization, and administrative restrictions. That disparity explains how the Israelis can depict the occupation as benign and beneficial, quoting statistics on the increase in GNP and the consumption of durables, while Palestinians can condemn it as exploitative, quoting statistics on terms of trade, differential subsidization, lack of credit, and usurpation of resources.

The Economic Structure and Israeli Control. The economic structure in the territories is an important element in the Israeli system of control. Israel controls all policy instruments absolutely and uses them to dispense favors to collaborators and to punish dissidents. Continued individual prosperity makes it hard to mobilize the masses for resistance. Personal affluence is tangible and cherished; communal stagnation is theoretical, therefore remote. Such manipulation of policy instruments is, however, a short-term and shortsighted device. Eventually, individual prosperity and improved education breed the resolve, and arouse people to the need, to struggle for communal and national development. Control, by definition, is a short-term concept. Lacking any clue for a long-term solution, the Israelis must satisfy themselves by perfecting their system of control.

The Palestinians, however, are also occupied with only short-term considerations. They could have vitalized their stagnated productive branches, even within the constraints of the unfavorable economic conditions. Personal prosperity has left them with considerable savings. There has been a constant decrease in the weight of private consumption (in local uses), from 79 percent in the early 1970s to 71 percent in the early 1980s, and an increase in investment,

from 9 percent to 22 percent. Yet private investment is directed predominantly to the construction of dwellings and not to investment in production generating assets. The Palestinians are insecure, disoriented, and intimidated, and their psychological environment is not conducive to the risk taking involved in long-term investments.

The Dual System. All things being equal, the short-term economic pattern of the dual system is set: migratory labor, stagnated production sector, lack of capital formation, minimal physical infrastructure, lack of support systems and administrative infrastructure, fragmentation, total dependence, brain drain of professionals, emigration of entrepreneurs and export of capital, proletarization of the peasantry and eventual urbanization—all of these elements combined with relative prosperity. In other words, the dual system is bound to form a Palestinian "eth-class" in the territories that will unite with the exisiting Palestinian eth-class on the other side of the Green Line, the Israeli Arabs.

Israeli economic policies can be viewed from the perspective of sixteen years of occupation as well thought out, coherent, and consistent. The dual system that emerged seems to indicate a grand design. It is argued that the premeditated objectives of the economic policies were to subjugate the Palestinian economy, to destroy its viability, to create economic hardships that would induce emigration (especially of men in their prime, the educated, and the professionals), to exploit the natural and human resources of the territories, and thus to facilitate Jewish settlement and eventual annexation.

In view of the haphazard, inconsistent, and low-level economic decision-making process concerning the territories, however, the "grand design" theory seems far-fetched. All the major decisions shaping the economic history of the occupation were taken on the spur of the moment, as a reaction to immediate pressures, usually by politicians who did not perceive the long-term implication of their decisions or by low-level bureaucrats who lacked high-level guidance. In hindsight these decisions were placed in a coherent framework by friends and foes alike. The open bridges policy with Jordan, the employment of laborers in Israel, the negotiations on the reopening of Jordanian and foreign banks, the allocation of development budgets, and the cancellation of credit facilities are but a few examples of the low-level and unplanned economic decision making. The economic issue of the territories has never been considered a vital problem that needed proper planning and top-level decision-making guidance. The economic aspect was subsumed (like other aspects of policies concerning the territories) in the general issue of control. Economic policies and practices were always subject to the overriding "security considerations."

The short-term, inconsistent approach was nevertheless based on a more coherent and fundamental notion that the Israeli side should be the only dynamic force, whereas the Palestinians were to be basically static, easily manipulated. The lack of a grand design does not mean that the policies adopted were accidental. As we shall see elsewhere (see the section "Land Seized by Declaring It 'State Land'"), Israelis perceive themselves as the only legitimate collective in the land of Israel, and therefore all Palestinian claims to communal (economic and political) rights are illegitimate and, by definition, subversive. This view, though diffused and controversial among Israelis ideologically, served as an unwritten guideline for economic decision makers.

Operatively the guideline can be summarized thus: We should not develop the economy of the territories, but we should not object to the improvement of the standard of living there. Development would cause competition with Israeli products. By gaining economic independence, subversive elements would achieve political power that would enable them to further their objective: the creation of a Palestinian state—a political and security risk for Israel. A reasonable standard of living can be achieved by employment in Israel, which, on the one hand, will increase dependence on Israel and, on the other hand, will diminish national aspirations. Economic dependence should be enhanced by interconnecting all grids (roads, electricity, communication, water) and by forcing the territories to use only Israeli ports for import and export. Economic measures should be an integral element in the carrot-and-stick policy of the military government. We can see how a dual system, neither preconceived nor well defined, could nevertheless emerge from these practical guidelines.

Agriculture

Stability and Productivity. Agriculture is the most important, stable, and productive branch of the West Bank economy. Its relative importance and productivity are manifest in the following indexes and indicators.[1]

The gross national product deriving from agriculture has fluctuated around the 30 percent mark since 1968. It reached 34.8 percent in 1968 and 29.2 percent in 1980. Fluctuations (some of them quite strong, for example, to 21.9 percent in 1977, to 22 percent in 1979) were caused in part by climatic conditions but even more by the strong influence of West Bank labor on the GNP. Isolating GNP emanating from labor in Israel by measuring the share of agriculture in the gross domestic product shows how stable that branch

has remained over time. Agriculture in the total GDP of the West Bank was 35.1 percent in 1970, 36.2 percent in 1975, 31.4 percent in 1977, and 35.0 percent in 1980. The third indicator, the number of workers employed in agriculture, shows a definite decline from 42 percent of the West Bank labor force in 1968 to 30 percent in 1980. The GNP emanating from agriculture in Gaza shows a clear decline from 28.1 percent in 1968 to 12.3 percent in 1980, and the share of GDP shows a decline from 28.4 percent in 1968 to 19.2 percent in 1980. The decline in the percentage of the labor force employed in agriculture in Gaza is sharper than in the West Bank. It dropped from 33 percent in 1969 to 18.2 percent in 1980.

The annual average rate of increase in real terms of agricultural production was 9.6 percent in the West Bank and 6.1 percent in Gaza (1968–1981). The annual rates of growth in value added were 9.2 percent and 6.3 percent in the West Bank and Gaza, respectively (1967–1981). The index of value of production (1968 = 100) reached 329.3 in 1981 in the West Bank and 216.2 in Gaza.

The value-added index (1968 = 100) reached 314.4 in 1981 in the West Bank and 221.9 in Gaza. Index of value added per worker (1968 = 100) reached 463.2 in 1981 in the West Bank and 369.6 in Gaza.

The ratio of output to labor indicates productivity. Before 1967 agriculture contributed about a quarter of the total GNP in the West Bank and provided one-half of all employment. This ratio indicates low productivity in the Jordanian period. During the post-1967 period an output/labor ratio emerged indicating a substantial increase in productivity. Productivity per worker doubled between 1967 and 1973 in the West Bank and rose rapidly in Gaza until the late 1970s.

Intensification. The increased productivity was due to changes in the methods of cultivation, to increased mechanization, to technological innovations and investment in expertise and human capital, to a drop in disguised unemployment, to phasing out of marginal cultivable areas, and to the replacement of low-value crops with high-value cash crops.

One indicator that measures the degree of intensification is the value of purchased inputs as a percentage of the value of production. This ratio rose from 10 percent in 1970–1972 to 18 percent in 1973–1975 and then dropped to 14 percent in 1980. The average annual figure for purchased input (1968–1980) was 16.7 percent in the West Bank and 33 percent in Gaza (the higher figure was mainly due to citrus-packing material). In Israel, by comparison, the ratio is 48 percent. The use of fertilizers per dunam rose from 2.3 kilograms per dunam in 1968–1969 to 9.5 kilograms per dunam in 1979–1980.(A dunam is a

TABLE 4
DUNAMS UNDER CULTIVATION IN THE WEST BANK, 1966–1981
(thousands)

Type of Land and Crop	1966	1968	1973	1974	1975	1976	1980	1981
Total irrigated land	100	57	82	81	83	89	92	98
Field crops	—	—	—	—	—	—	14	16
Vegetables and potatoes	74	31	54	53	56	61	49	50
Watermelons	—	—	—	—	—	—	—	2
Citrus	24	24	25	24	24	25	25	25
Bananas and miscellaneous	2	2	3	4	3	3	`4	5
Total rain-fed land	1,980	1,988	1,941	1,939	1,878	1,931	1,859	1,909
Field crops	850	833	827	709	538	693	521	528
Watermelons	71	43	10	5	3	5	12	35
Vegetables	110	70	16	110	101	41	34	49
Fruit trees, including olives	949	680	738	801	901	812	957	962
Fallow	—	362	350	314	335	380	335	335
Total	2,080	2,045	2,023	2,020	1,961	2,020	1,951	2,007
Total, excluding fallow	2,080	1,683	1,673	1,706	1,626	1,640	1,616	1,672

NOTE: Dashes indicate fewer than 500.
SOURCE: David Kahan, "Agriculture and Water in the West Bank and Gaza," West Bank Data Base Project, May 1983, tables 8, 9.

unit of land area equal to 1,000 square meters or about one-quarter acre.) The number of tractors increased from 185 in 1968–1969 to 1,883 in 1979–1980 and in Gaza from 12 to 636.

Income. As a result of the increased productivity, there was a substantial increase in the income of rural families and consequently in their standard of living. The average income per capita of the rural population was $666 in 1974 and $930 in 1975 (West Bank), compared with $133 in 1966. The nutritional value of the food consumed was estimated in 1964–1966 at 2,430 calories per day (11.5 grams/day of animal protein, 51 grams/day of fats). In 1979 the nutritional value was estimated at 2,833 calories per day (21.1 grams/day of animal protein, 70.8 grams/day of fats). In Gaza the nutritional value of food rose from an estimated 2,091 calories per day (1969–1971) to 2,386 (1975–1977). By comparison, the Israeli (1979) food basket is estimated at 3,039 calories/day (24.9 grams/day proteins, 113.5 grams/day fats) and Jordan's food basket (1977) at 2,067 calories. The increase in the standard of living of rural families is demonstrated by the general improvement in housing and in the purchase of durable goods. It should be borne in mind, however, that the improvement in the standard of living of rural families is caused to a large extent by wages of members of the families employed in Israel.

The Resource Base. It is significant that the progress in agricultural production and increased productivity has been achieved without any radical change in the resource base. Since 1967 there have been no marked changes in the overall cultivated areas, either in Gaza or in the West Bank. Table 4 shows the breakdown of cultivated land in the West Bank; table 5 does the same for Gaza.

Irrigated land as a percentage of total cultivated land has increased in the West Bank by a mere one percentage point (1966–1981). In Gaza the increase in

TABLE 5
DUNAMS UNDER CULTIVATION IN THE GAZA REGION, 1966–1979
(thousands)

	1966	1967–1968	1974–1975	1978–1979
Total cultivated area	187	204	210	210
Rain-fed crops	112	114	115	115
Irrigated crops	75	90	95	95
Perennial crops	119	118	126	128
Annual crops	68	86	84	82

SOURCE: Kahan, "Agriculture," table 5.

irrigated land as a percentage of total cultivated land was five percentage points; the figure rose from 40 percent in 1966 to 45 percent in 1978–1979.

Both public and private investment in agriculture remained very low throughout the period. In the mid-1970s, with increased prosperity, there was some investment in mechanization, mainly in tractors, trucks, and water pipes. Most of it, however, was financed from the farmers' own resources through business savings. Military government loans never exceeded 10 percent of the total investment in the branch. Loans to agriculture ceased altogether in the late 1970s. There is no capital market or credit system. The development budget of the military government, which was minimal (except between 1969 and 1972), was canceled altogether in 1981. Regular budgets have fallen in real terms since 1970–1971. There has been a marked drop in the budget directed to research and agricultural experiments. In 1967 there were 133 senior field advisers. By 1982 their number had dropped to 65. No organizational framework to undertake investment in regional infrastructure was set up. No organized regional marketing system has been established. Marketing remains in the hands of a few large-scale local wholesalers in the urban centers of each area. The reduction of the labor force in agriculture as a result of employment in Israel did not initially affect production, but it eliminated disguised unemployment. Since the mid-1970s, however, labor productivity in agriculture began to even out in the West Bank and to fall in Gaza, suggesting that labor scarcity had become in the late 1970s an effective constraint on production. No changes were instituted in land tenure or in other structural and organizational support systems.

Development Strategies. The minimal changes in the resource base and support systems reflect a clear Israeli development strategy. The strategy was termed "improvement" as opposed to "transformation." The improvement strategy is characterized by the initiation of change within the existing resource base and infrastructure rather than by efforts to transform the rural infrastructure through heavy capital expenditure, land reform, a move to processing of produce, and improved structural support systems. Improvements in agriculture were attempted "without relying on the dynamics of development that would have emerged from changing structural patterns." The official assessment of the strategy read: "The transfer of modern technology and the evolution of an appropriate market operated not only to neutralize the restraining effects of a conservative structure, but also to initiate a chain reaction of accelerating development at a rate the region had never known before."[2] Viewed as improvement, agricultural development in

the post-1967 years has been substantial. We might argue, however, that it is false to compare agricultural development over time, taking an existing resource and structural base and a very low starting point, namely the pre-1967 situation. It can be convincingly claimed that changes can be measured only against the alternative strategy, that of transformation.

Implicit in the improvement strategy are a freeze on the agricultural resources available to the Arab population and complete Israeli control over growth potential. Arab agriculture was allowed to develop as long as its development would not compete or interfere with Israeli interests or put a fiscal and economic burden on the Israeli system. The "appropriate market forces" were allowed to operate only when they were harnessed to the Israeli economy and were beneficial to it.

Water. The natural resource base has not changed. Despite claims that Israeli land expropriation has created a land shortage, arable land seems not to be a constraint on development. The shortage of land suitable for high-value crops under irrigation, however, is a major constraint. Such land is situated in the Jordan Valley and is totally taken for Israeli agricultural production. Water consumption for agriculture had been frozen at a level 20 percent higher than in 1967. Of some 500,000 dunams of land potentially irrigable for agricultural use, fewer than 100,000 dunams actually are irrigated. The additional 200–300 million cubic meters of water required must be taken from existing or planned Jewish settlements on both sides of the Green Line. Of the "shared water resources" of Israel and the West Bank, only 25 percent are used by West Bank Palestinian residents (113 million cubic meters). Shared water resources are estimated at 460 million cubic meters of almost 2 billion cubic meters of total resources of Western Palestine (23 percent). By 1990 water consumption by West Bank Palestinians is planned at 137 million cubic meters, or 6.3 percent of the total for Western Palestine—the same ratio as in 1976. According to a strict policy, licenses for drilling in the West Bank are refused. The official explanation is that "increased productivity can take place by improved on-farm irrigation methods." It is clear that West Bank farmers are being forced to maintain extensive rather than intensive agriculture and to develop traditional agricultural branches. The fact that they must rely almost exclusively on rainfall puts them at the mercy of climatic conditions. Drought years and seasonal fluctuations in fruit yield (especially of olives) cause unexpected drops in production.

Consequences. The lack of a regional marketing structure and the total dependence on Israeli (and to some extent Jordanian) trade policies put Palestinian farmers at the mercy of outside forces on which they have no influence. Consequently there is serious market uncertainty. Whenever West Bank and Gaza agricultural production becomes a threat to Israeli farmers, the government takes steps to protect the interest of the Israeli farmers. Between 1967 and 1971 shipments of vegetables from the West Bank were restricted. The marketing in Israel of West Bank plums and grapes is prohibited. The cultivation of winter tomatoes and cucumbers by Palestinian farmers caused a sharp drop in the revenue of Israeli farmers, and as a result a quota system was introduced in Order 1039. The Israeli official view is that the restrictions and quotas are aimed at achieving the better planning and marketing of produce, which will eventually increase the revenue of Palestinian farmers. The planning seems to take into account the economic and political interest of Israeli farmers, however, and not that of the Palestinian farmers. Produce planning in Israel is based on an elaborate system of minimum price guarantees and subsidies, and Israeli agriculture has a highly developed system of supports (marketing and credit). Palestinian farmers, not enjoying these conditions, are faced with unfair competition. On the one hand, they are integrated into the Israeli system and must adjust to its market conditions; on the other hand, they are excluded from its system of supports.

The alternative marketing outlet, the open bridges with Jordan, is economically important. Agricultural trade with Jordan, however, has maintained only the pre-1967 level. As in industry, such agricultural trade did not contribute to economic growth in the territories. Jordanian trade policies have recently been changed to protect the thriving agricultural sector in the East Jordan Valley. It is clear that the Palestinians in the West Bank and Gaza are caught between the Israeli hammer and the Jordanian anvil. Both sovereign states maintain trade policies aimed at benefiting their own populations. Palestinian farmers are treated by the two countries as both indigenous and alien, whichever view suits each state's self-interest at any given time.

The Palestinians' total dependence on Israeli economic conditions is illustrated by sweeping changes in the rate of agricultural growth before and after 1975. During the initial period rapid growth was achieved. In the West Bank between the years 1967 and 1970, the average annual rate of growth was 11.4 percent in value of agricultural production, 11.3 percent in value added, and 15.8 percent in value added per worker; in Gaza the figures were 8.8 percent, 9.4 percent, and 13.6 percent, respectively. Between 1979 and 1981, the annual growth rate dropped dramatically: the West Bank saw a 4.9 percent increase in value of production, a 6.0 percent increase in value

added, and an 8.0 increase in value added per worker; in Gaza the figures were 0.9 percent, 1.3 percent, and 6.9 percent, respectively. The differential growth rate corresponds to the general growth rates of the West Bank and Gaza economies. Until the mid-1970s the average growth rate of GNP was 14 percent, slowing to 7 percent in the latter part of the period. These changes reflect the dynamics of the Israeli economy, which went from an initial period of rapid growth in the early 1970s to a much slower rate of growth in the late 1970s and early 1980s.

Policies of "improvement" have chained Palestinian agriculture to Israeli economic fortunes, and the link has had detrimental effects when the Israeli economy has performed poorly. The high growth rates in the initial period, moreover, reflect the economic dynamics of transition from the pre-1967 conditions rather than performance sustainable over a longer period. The "evolution of an appropriate market" envisaged by Israeli planners apparently did not create a chain reaction strong enough to sustain accelerated development. Because the alternative strategy of transformation, which requires changes in "structural patterns," was not implemented, we cannot determine whether the dynamic of development that it was meant to produce would have been more sustainable.

The existing economic interaction between the territories and Israel brought benefits to Palestinian agriculture in a largely rural economy with a low level of technology that lacked a functional organizational support system. It can be argued, however, that the relationship between the two entities, though possessing innumerable benefits, created a situation of economic dependency. Agricultural production receives little protection, and any opportunities that do emerge tend to be controlled by the richer economy. The benefits accrued from interaction with the Israeli territories have been unevenly distributed. They flow to the economically stronger side at the expense of the weaker.

Industry in the West Bank

Basic Data. The rapid growth in per capita income in the West Bank was not accompanied by comparable growth in the industrial sector. Contrary to normal patterns of growth, industrial production has declined. The industrial sector's contribution to the gross domestic product fell from 9.0 percent in 1968 to 8.2 percent in 1975 and 6.5 percent in 1980. The West Bank economy may be described as nonindustrialized. With GNP per capita twice as high as in Egypt, the West Bank's industrial contribution to GDP is a quarter of the Egyptian industrial contribution. Productivity, measured by value added per worker in industry, was less than half the value added per worker in agriculture in 1980. The total number of people employed in industry has remained at approximately 15,000 since 1970; 22 percent are employed in olive processing, 18 percent in textiles, 18 percent in quarrying, 10 percent in the food industry, 4–6 percent in metallurgy (locksmiths), and 14 percent in carpentry, tailoring, and miscellaneous workshops. Of almost 2,000 plants, 60 employ more than 20 workers, and only 3 employ more than 100 workers. Of the industrial work force, 23 percent reside in the Nablus subdistrict, 20 percent in Hebron, 18 percent in Ramallah–el Bira, 16 percent in the Bethlehem-Jericho subdistrict, and 10 percent in Jenin.[3]

Growth Rates. In absolute rather than relative terms, there has been modest growth in the industrial sector. Growth in value added is estimated at an average annual rate of 4.5 percent, compared with an average growth of 7 percent in Israeli industry and almost 8 percent in Jordanian industry. This average growth rate, however, should be broken down to three distinct business cycles during the 1970s and early 1980s: (1) a comparatively high growth rate in the early years; (2) a sharp downturn in the middle of the decade; and (3) a moderate, short-term rebound at the end of the 1970s. There is a clear correlation between the West Bank industrial growth and Israeli business cycles. Growth in the Israeli economy has meant growth in the West Bank industry. This correspondence points to the critical dependence of West Bank industry on the Israeli economy. Moreover, available data suggest that in recent years the West Bank industrial sector was unable to take advantage of growth in either the Israeli or the West Bank economy, a development that called the viability of the industrial sector, such as it is, into question.

Outlets. The West Bank domestic market is the primary outlet for West Bank industrial products. More than twice as many products manufactured in the West Bank were sold to the domestic market as were sold to Israel excluding Jerusalem. This disparity indicates the existence of a segmented market.

There is little penetration of the Jewish market by West Bank finished retail goods, except in shoes, textiles, and, to some extent, furniture. In building products, quarrying, stone dressing, and grinding, there is a substantial Israeli market for West Bank products. Subcontracting in footwear, clothing, and carpentry, accounting for 12 percent of the total industrial revenue in the 1970s, has shown signs of decline in recent years.

The third market for West Bank industry, Jordan, has been greatly restricted. Total West Bank exports to Jordan in 1981 did not significantly differ from those in 1970. Jordanian government policy is in a way a continuation, though in different forms, of the institutionalized discrimination of the pre-1967 years. Data on the origin of exports and the type of goods exported suggest that there has been a continuing attempt to freeze the structure of industry as it existed in 1966, that is, to favor those few firms that were established with Jordanian assistance during their rule. These firms are chocolate, samna (liquid margarine), and plastic factories. Of 201 firms sampled in the West Bank, only 12 percent exported goods to Jordan. Jordan prohibits imports of textiles, stone and tiles, detergents, and pharmaceuticals, ostensibly to maintain the Arab boycott but in fact to protect infant Jordanian industries.

An overall assessment of the role of the three markets—domestic, Israeli, and Jordanian—does not inspire optimism. The growing gap in workers' productivity between Israeli and West Bank industry will have negative effects on West Bank sales to Israel. Sales to the Jordanian market will continue to fall as consumption of traditional goods and Nablusian soap drops. The sole hope is the domestic market, but in this market, too, local products will face increased difficulties with the improved standard of living. It is highly doubtful whether growing domestic consumption will offset the decline in sales in the other two markets. West Bank industry, like agriculture, is caught between the Israeli hammer and the Jordanian anvil.

The Effects of Israeli Policies. The Israeli economic policies of "integration and exclusion" are more pronounced in industry than in any other economic sphere. In Israel government involvement in industry is massive, occurring through selective taxation, subsidies, and investment. In the last decade government investment has accounted for 50 percent of gross capital formation in Israeli industry. The government is directly involved in refinancing, and its agencies are the dominant actors in infrastructural development.

In the West Bank, by contrast, local industry receives no government assistance, no development of infrastructure, and no subsidies, credit, or any other form of support. Moreover, in recent years, West Bank industry has been forced to compete with Israeli plants built in close proximity in the new settlements.

The differential treatment has become ethnically rather than geographically defined. Under such circumstances, Palestinian industrial growth is not likely to occur, since it is dependent on, and is controlled by, two industrial sectors—Israel and Jordan—that are developing very fast. It is likely that even the meager growth so far achieved will be wiped out.

I do not mean that the industrialization of the

West Bank will not take place. All signs show that the region will undergo rapid industrial development. The industrialization, however, will be Jewish, not Arab.

Jewish Industries in the West Bank. By 1983 six Jewish industrial parks had been constructed in the West Bank:

Shaked (Samaria)	40 dunams
Barkan (Samaria)	300 dunams
Maaleh Ephraim (Jordan Highlands)	70 dunams
Karnei Shomron (Samaria)	150 dunams
Maaleh Adumim (Judea)	650 dunams
Kiryat Arba (Judea)	50 dunams
Total	1,260 dunams

In the operating plants some 2,500 workers are employed, 70 percent of whom are Jewish. The largest park is Maaleh Adumim, on the Jerusalem-Jericho highway. Established in 1975 under the Rabin government, it employs 800–1,000 workers. Half are Jewish workers employed in military installations. The other half are predominantly Arabs employed in some eighty firms. The private firms are small, labor-intensive establishments similar to Arab industries in the West Bank: they produce sewing, food, aluminum, and building materials. The industrial park of Kiryat Arba (near Hebron), also established before 1977, has the same small-scale, labor-intensive character, and more than half the employees are Arabs.

The current policies of the authorities are to build only capital-intensive, sophisticated factories to achieve two objectives: to minimize the need for settlers to commute to the cities and to limit Arab employment. The new industrial park of Barkan (near Ariel in Western Samaria) is an example: strict criteria have been established for capital investment, for the proportion of Jewish and Arab labor, and for construction timetables. More than twenty companies have already received approval, and there is a long waiting list. Government assistance to West Bank Jewish industries is massive. The region is classified as Development Area A+ and A (depending on the distance from the Green Line and on other considerations). This status makes West Bank Jewish industries eligible for grants of 30 percent and loans of 40 percent of their investment at a real interest rate of 0.5 percent or, linked to the dollar, of 6 percent. Plants are entitled to free physical infrastructure and to short-term credit facilities.

Planned Industrial Development. Israeli plans for industrialization of the West Bank (part of the *Plan of Hundred Thousand Settlers*, World Zionist Organization, 1982) call for the establishment of seven additional industrial parks. The total area designated for

industrial parks in the West Bank by 2010 is 15,010 dunams. For Jewish industrial workers 83,500 jobs will be created, and for Arabs 25,000.

In the short term, by 1986, an additional 8,750 Jewish and 2,200 Arab industrial jobs will be created. Investment in the new Jewish industrial parks is estimated at $250 million over five years ($60–100 million for infrastructure and the rest for 70 percent government equity participation). Compared with the existing investment in Jewish industry in the West Bank ($328 million) and government participation in industrial gross capital formation in 1981 alone ($400 million), an investment of $50 million a year seems modest. The total area for industrial development for the target year 2010 appears in table 6.

TABLE 6
AREAS PLANNED FOR INDUSTRIAL DEVELOPMENT IN 2010
(dunams)

Region	Land
Existing 1983	1,260
North Samaria	
Shaked	240
Teretz	560
Central Samaria	
Shomronit	800
Karnei Shomron	600
Barkan	600
Beit Arieh	600
Maaleh Ephraim	2,400
Jerusalem area	
Atarot-jaba	2,000
Maaleh Adumin	3,200
Rimonim	500
Teqo'a	400
Hebron area	
Kiryat Arba	850
Carmel	500
Local industrial zones	500
Total	15,010

SOURCE: Author.

Three types of industrial zones are envisaged. Small industrial parks contiguous to residential communities and based exclusively on sophisticated technology will, it is hoped, reduce commuting among Jews and prevent the employment of Arabs. All other industry will be located in either regional or interregional parks within fifteen miles of the main Jewish urban concentrations. The industrialization plan, designed to meet almost 20 percent of the total industrial needs of Israel, is ambitious and has the potential to succeed, at least as far as the major industrial parks are concerned. These parks are situated within a radius of fifteen miles from Israel's industrial belt

(Ashdod-Hadera). They are eligible for assistance at the highest level, despite the short distance from the existing industrial zones that receive no assistance. Moving to the new industrial parks in the West Bank entitles entrepreneurs not only to receive massive financing but also to sell their old property in the urban center at a high profit and to receive a free plot with a sophisticated physical infrastructure. Industrial development in the West Bank is an integral part of the Israeli suburbanization strategy, as we shall see. It continues the process of suburbanization within the central region eastward that started in the early 1970s. This process is likely to accelerate because of enormous government incentives. It means not only easier access to work for the Jewish settlers in the West Bank but also a gradual suburbanization of industry itself within the West Bank.

The Effects on the Arab Population. Of the total work force planned for the Jewish industry in the West Bank (108,000), 25,000 are Arabs. The planners anticipate a very low proportion of Arab workers, since most of the planned industries are high technology and capital intensive, employing small numbers of blue-collar workers. Moreover, high-technology plants are usually defense related and are therefore closed to Arab employment. Although 25,000 Arab workers constitute a mere 23 percent of the total planned employment, the figure is almost double the existing Palestinian industrial labor force in the territories. These additional workers will be drawn mainly from the present commuters to industrial plants within the Green Line but also from farmers in the West Bank. Jewish industrialization of the West Bank is likely to accelerate proletarianization.

The industrialization plan describes present policies of the government vis-à-vis Arab industry as "non-policies—ignoring Arab industrial trends, and lack of interest." The plan recommends that the government continue with the existing policies of *no* "participation, financing and investment" in the Arab sector. The plan calls for "restricting industrial development in the urban centers of Nablus, Ramallah, Tul Karm, Jenin, Bethlehem, Jericho, Hebron [to] prevent the development of [Arab] industrial areas near the urban center" and thereby to prevent "to a certain degree" the growth of Arab cities.[4] According to the plan, Arab incentives should be dispersed outside the urban centers, and the development of small-scale workshop areas in villages should be encouraged. Arab industries would be allowed to establish industrial sites in the Jewish parks, but they would not be eligible for Israeli incentives. This recommendation is unlikely to elicit much response from Palestinian industrialists. The stagnant Arab industry, lacking any assistance, will find the potential costs too high and the potential advantages negligible.

Notes

1. The data are based on David Kahan, "Agriculture and Water in the West Bank and Gaza," mimeographed (Jerusalem: West Bank Data Base Project, 1983).
2. Shmuel Pohorylis, "The Development of Agriculture in the Administered Territories," mimeographed (Tel Aviv: Ministry of Agriculture, February 1976), pp. 8, 9.
3. Industrial data are based on Hillel Frisch, *Stagnation and Frontier: Arab and Jewish Industry in the West Bank* (Jerusalem: West Bank Data Base Project, forthcoming).
4. World Zionist Organization, "Jewish Industry: A Master Plan and Development Plan for Industrial Estates" (Jerusalem, 1982), p. 8.

3
Alienated Islands: Land Use

The bitter Israeli-Palestinian struggle for the territories is encapsulated in the battle for land control. This is the true area of the binational conflict: land ownership, land use, physical planning, settlements, irrigation, afforestation, roads, and utility grids. Even single dwellings are perceived in wide, national terms, like military operations. The rocky hills, fertile valleys, and desolate wilderness transcend their intrinsic value and are revered as symbolic objects with almost spiritual significance. Nowhere in the modern world is the concept of *patria* so intimately felt as in the lands west of the Jordan.

Redemption of the land (*geulat haqarqa*) is a fundamental Zionist concept loaded with supreme symbolic and ideological significance. It is land that the Jewish people sought to liberate. The national conflict with the Palestinians was perceived as a conflict not between equal peoples but between one legitimate collective and a local population that happened to be squatting on that land. The history of the Zionist enterprise is an account of physical *faits accomplis* through land acquisition and settlement, created to achieve national, political, and military objectives. Most Israelis perceive the occupation of the territories as a direct continuation of the Zionist enterprise. The policies of "land reclamation" are therefore vigorously pursued.

The Palestinians, attaching the same macronational and symbolic value to the land, resist Israeli land acquisition efforts with whatever means they can muster. The unequal strength of the conflicting parties, however, dictates the results. The Israelis, backed by the full coercive power of a sovereign state and by vast material resources, succeed through a variety of methods in attaining their objectives and in gaining control over more and more areas. The scramble for space, however, is far from being decided totally in favor of the Israelis. One Palestinian reaction to Israeli takeover efforts has been unprecedented building activity and fruit-tree planting, which has at least se-cured enough space to allow uninterrupted population growth.

Although the battle for the land is still raging, it is already possible to predict its outcome. The Israelis are in the process of gaining direct control over 40 percent of the West Bank land mass and 31 percent of the Gaza Strip area. The Palestinians will probably be able to retain at least limited control over 3.2 million dunams in the West Bank and 250,000 dunams in Gaza (58 percent and 69 percent, respectively). To understand the meaning of those figures, we should bear in mind that thirty-seven years ago, in 1947, the Jews possessed less than 10 percent of the total land of Mandatory Palestine. In 1983 they possessed 85 percent of the area, and the Palestinians (including Israeli Arabs) controlled less than 15 percent.

Tables 7, 8, and 9 present all the available information on land use, both existing and planned, in the West Bank and Gaza. There is no comprehensive planning process in the territories except sectarian Israeli planning. Therefore information on land use must be culled from various sources. Conflicting information must be reconciled, sometimes by conjecture. I am satisfied, however, with the degree of consistency achieved. The tables should be read in conjunction with maps 4, 5, 6, and 7 in this book. Table 7 enables us to compare Jewish and Arab land use in the West Bank, with respect both to total control and to particular types of land use. Table 8 summarizes the percentages of land use types according to ethnic group in the West Bank; table 9 does the same for Gaza. The appendix at the end of this chapter lists the sources and methods of computation and charting.

Built-up Areas

Jewish Areas. The Jewish planned built-up area in the West Bank amounts to 6.6 percent of the total area in direct Israeli possession. This low figure reflects the

TABLE 7

LAND USE IN THE WEST BANK, BY TYPE AND ETHNIC DISTRIBUTION, EXISTING AND PLANNED, 1983
(thousands of dunams)

Use of Land	Jewish			Arab			Total
	Existing	Planned	Total	Existing	Planned	Total	
Built-up areas	42.0	100.0	142.0	140.0	120.0[a]	260.0	402.0
Roads, right of way	—	—	—	—	—	—	140.0[b]
Industry	1.25	13.75	15.0	[c]	—	—	15.0
Agriculture	45.0	55.0	100.0	1,400.0	− 120.0[a]	1,280.0	1,380.0
Grazing, fallow, marginally cultivated	5.0	140.0	145.0	1,745.0	− 140.0[d]	1,605.0	1,750.0
Restricted area (mil.)[e]	1,150.0	0	1,150.0	0	0	0	1,150.0
Nature reserves	250.0	90.0	340.0	0	0	0	340.0
Total excluding roads	1,493.25	398.75	1,892.0	3,285.0	− 140.0	3,145.0	5,037.0
Total including roads	—	—	—	—	—	—	5,177.0
Reserve land use	—	—	258.0[f]	—	—	65.0	323.0
Total area in possession	—	—	2,150.0[g]	—	—	3,210.0	5,500.0[h]
Dead Sea water surface	—	—	—	—	—	—	300.0
Total area	—	—	—	—	—	—	5,800.0

NOTE: Dashes indicate that data are unavailable or inapplicable.
a. Agriculture to be changed to built-up.
b. Pre-1967, 1,400 km at 50 meters; post-1967, 800 km at 100 meters (50 and 100 meters refer to average road widths for rights-of-way).
c. Included in built-up.
d. Taken by Jewish grazing.
e. Some overlap of grazing and nature reserve.
f. Difference between land use and "state land" area.
g. Excluding roads.
h. Including roads.
SOURCES: Maps and notes to chapters 3 and 4, and appendix to chapter 3.

new Israeli settlement strategy of high-density urban and suburban housing. New towns are planned with gross housing density of two family units per dunam. Towns such as Ariel in Central Samaria are planned for 35,000 families on a gross area of 16,000 dunams. Smaller urban centers such as Kedumim and Bethel are planned for 10,000 families on 5,000 dunams. Garden suburbs and rural settlements are planned for lower density, but their total built-up area is relatively small. In the West Bank 132 planned rural settlements are planned to occupy 42 percent of the Jewish built-up area and include 17.5 percent of the total population. The total Jewish built-up area is designed to accommodate a Jewish population of 600,000–800,000 by 2010. The existing detailed physical plans, now being implemented, use slope gradients of 25 percent in rural settlements and 50 percent in urban centers. The detached and semidetached housing estates are quite congested by U.S. suburban standards but are reasonable by Israeli standards. There is no reason to challenge the Israeli planners' assertion that no more space is needed for housing beyond the planned

142,000 dunams. In some areas considered essential for settlement, however, no "state land" is available. Therefore Israeli planners seek to purchase land from Arab owners. The area planned for purchase is 31,500 dunams.

Jewish population density in the Gaza Strip is very low. The total number of Jewish families planned for Gaza is 1,750–2,000 (7,000–8,000 persons) on an area of 113,000 dunams. One urban center and ten rural settlements are planned for the area.[1]

Arab Areas. Arab built-up areas and sprawl deserve close scrutiny because Arab building activity seems to be the most effective way of resisting Israeli land seizure. The first impression conveyed by map 1, showing Arab built-up areas, is the very high ratio of built-up area to other land uses (8.1 percent) in a basically rural society (70 percent of the population resides in villages). This impression emanates from the fact that the modern building pattern of Arabs is very extensive, involving "ribbon development" (long and narrow built-up areas on both sides of access roads) and

TABLE 8
LAND USE IN THE WEST BANK, BY ETHNIC GROUP,
EXISTING AND PLANNED, 1983
(percent)

	Total Land Mass	Jewish	Arab
Built-up areas	7.3	6.6	8.1
Roads	2.5	—	—
Industry	0.3	0.7	—
Agriculture	25.1	4.7	39.9
Grazing	31.8	6.7	50.0
Restricted areas	20.9	53.5	—
Nature reserve	6.2	15.8	—
Reserve, unknown	5.9	12.0	2.0
Total	100.0	100.0	100.0
% of total land mass	100.0	39.1[a]	58.4[a]

NOTE: Total land mass = 5.50 million dunams. Total Jewish land mass = 2.15 million dunams. Total Arab land mass = 3.21 million dunams. Dashes indicate that data are unavailable or inapplicable.
a. Roads account for the extra 2.5%, or 140,000 dunams.
SOURCE: Table 7.

single-family houses interspersed with large tracts of orchards and farmsteads. This pattern is particularly noticeable in the Hebron-Halhul and Ramallah-Birzeit areas. Consequently the building density in the

TABLE 9
LAND USE IN THE GAZA STRIP, BY ETHNIC GROUP, 1983
(dunams)

	Area[a]
Arab	
Built-up areas	50,000
Agriculture and roads	200,000
Total Arab land use	250,000
Jewish	
Jewish settlements	32,300
Afforestation	10,000
Army camps	1,900
New roads (to settlements)	11,600
Leased to B'nai Shimon regional council (Israeli)	31,000
Leased to Gaza regional council	27,000
Total Jewish land use	113,800
Total Gaza Strip	363,800

NOTE: Approximately 105,000 dunams fall under state domain (most of it registered) and absentee ownership, not including expropriation for international borders, terminals, and so on.
a. Approximate.
SOURCE: Military Government (Gaza), Annual Reports.

"built-up sphere of influence" determined by the project is very low, estimated on the average to be 0.5 families per dunam.[2] The gross density is misleading, however, because at least 40 percent of the sphere of influence marked on the map (260,000 dunams) is used for agriculture. The actual built-up area is estimated at 140,000 dunams, and the average gross density at 0.8 families per dunam. It is assumed that the agricultural areas within the built-up sphere of influence will gradually be converted to housing. This has been the pattern of Arab housing development since 1967. In 1977, for example, the total built-up area in the Hebron planning zone was 7,000 dunams of 73,000 dunams, or 9.6 percent, the rest being used as orchards and farms. In 1982 the built-up area exceeded 20,000 dunams (27 percent). The same process can be seen in the rural sections of Ramallah–el Bira and Bethlehem. In fact, we may detect two trends: the extension of housing activity to ever-increasing distances from the old nuclei of towns and villages and at the same time in-fill construction on empty plots and agricultural areas within the existing built-up areas. Both processes reflect the phenomenal building activity and sprawl in the West Bank, which constitute the only development effort in an otherwise stagnant economy.

Statistical data and field surveys highlight the building activity. Tables 10 and 11 summarize construction activity in the West Bank. The ratio of building starts to population between 1974 and 1980 was seventy-four square meters per person (compared with fifty-seven square meters per person in Israel). West Bank investment in fixed assets was directed mainly to construction: 1970–1971, 48 percent; 1975–1976, 60 percent; 1979–1980, 55 percent.

The contradictory trends in construction for private and public purposes should be emphasized. Private building starts in 1981 were fourteen times those in 1968. By contrast, public construction starts in 1981 were 13.6 percent of starts in 1968. There is a consistent decrease in construction for public purposes, which highlights the previously discussed difference between individual prosperity and communal stagnation. Field studies and aerial photos provide additional information on building activity. Between 1968 and 1979 the increase in the built-up area in selected localities reached the following proportions:

Beit Jallah	55 percent
Al Bira	67 percent
Bethlehem (rural)	125 percent
Ramallah (south)	76 percent
Salfit	162 percent
Hebron	185 percent
Beit Sahur	267 percent

In fact, the area from Ein Yabrud–Bethel (north of

TABLE 10
CONSTRUCTION ACTIVITY IN THE WEST BANK, 1968–1981
(thousands of square meters)

	1968	1976	1977	1978	1979	1980	1981
Construction starts							
Private	55.6	339.0	674.0	781.0	792.0	750.0	778.0
Public	11.0	8.0	9.0	6.0	5.5	4.0	1.5
Construction completed							
Private	31.8	567.9	623.1	649.4	716.6	736.2	684.4
Public	47.2	12.5	4.4	5.9	9.0	3.6	3.9

SOURCE: Central Bureau of Statistics.

Ramallah) in the north to al Khadr (south of Bethlehem) in the south, defined as the metropolitan area of Jerusalem, had by 1983 become a continuous built-up area covering some 500,000 dunams. To be sure, building activity has not been uniform. Generally speaking, Hebron, the Jerusalem area, and Nablus show higher building activity than other towns and villages. Population density is also not uniform. Incomplete data point to a density of persons per dunam of built-up area (sphere of influence) ranging from 12 in Bethlehem, 5.4 in Beit Jallah, 4.8 in Nablus, and 3.3 in Hebron to 1.5 in Jenin. If we take into account all major towns' built-up area (90,000 dunams) and total population (about 270,000), the gross density reaches 3.0 persons per dunam, or 330 square meters per person. It is interesting that the population density in the built-up areas of smaller towns and villages is only slightly lower (about 2.7 persons per dunam) than in larger towns. This similarity reflects the uniformity in the Arab housing pattern of low-density single-story dwellings and the lack of high-density multistory housing even in larger towns. The population densities in Arab built-up areas are low by any standard. Measured by families (6 persons per family), the gross density is 0.5 families per dunam, or a quarter of the planned Jewish density of two families per dunam. If we allow for the difference in family size (Jewish, 3.6 persons; Arab, 6

persons) and calculate densities of one family per dunam (160 square meters per person), we see that the Arab population can be doubled within the existing built-up areas without causing congestion. In some areas, however, and especially in Bethlehem, Nablus, Tul Karm, and Qalqiliya, there seems to be a need to expand the residential area.

It would seem to be in the interest of the Arab population to halt spatial expansion and to increase population densities. The existing pattern puts heavy stress on municipal and communal services and prevents the planning of a rational and efficient physical and social infrastructure. It also places an undue burden on communal interaction, which is already difficult, given the circumstances of occupation. Furthermore, unplanned residential expansion would result in the loss of tens of thousands of dunams of prime agricultural land (especially orchards). To the Palestinian community, however, all rational planning considerations seem secondary to building to forestall expropriation, which has overriding political significance. Moreover, the Palestinian community lacks a central planning authority, and the official military government planning bodies implement explicitly partisan Israeli planning policies.

Roads

The road network existing in the West Bank in 1967 resembled a fish bone. The historic watershed highway ran north-south through the center of the West Bank, and access roads ran laterally away from it to the east and west. After 1948 the east-west roads connecting the area with the coast became dead-end roads. The Jordanian army expanded the western access road system to facilitate troop movements to the armistice line. The only major road work done under the Jordanians was the Jerusalem-Amman highway and the Jerusalem-Ramallah dual carriageway. In the 1950s, as Jordan realigned its road system from an east-west (to Palestinian ports) to a north-south

TABLE 11
CONSTRUCTION OF APARTMENTS IN THE WEST BANK, 1979–1981

Year	Apartments Completed
1979	5,199
1980	4,960
1981	4,752

SOURCE: Central Bureau of Statistics.

(Aqaba-Syria-Lebanon) orientation, the local character of the West Bank road network became more pronounced. The standard for local roads improved, however, and 93 percent of the roads were paved.

Road planning after 1967 followed Israeli geostrategic concepts. Until the mid-1970s the prevailing geostrategic concept was the Allon Plan, which envisaged linear north-south links between the Jordan Valley and Israel proper and no major interconnection on the west. Therefore, north-south road axes were developed: the Jericho–Ein Gedi highway (along the Dead Sea coast), the Jordan Valley highway, and the Allon Road (Maaleh Adumim–Maaleh Ephraim). In the mid-1970s, with the growing realization that chances for a political solution based on partition were diminishing, the government started to create east-west links between the coast and the Jordan Valley: the trans-Judea and trans-Samaria roads, as well as a new northern highway from the coast to Jerusalem, were planned.

The Likud government, true to its geostrategic concept of annexing the whole area, abandoned the north-south strategy and stressed instead the complete integration of the West Bank road system into the Israeli system. The master plan for roads in the West Bank defines the following principles (in order of declining priority): (1) the integration of the Israeli national road network with that of the West Bank; (2) the opening up of areas for suburban demand by creating road axes from urban centers to these areas; (3) the enhancement of new areas by improving road standards and by "bypassing local population areas"; (4) the interconnection of new settlement blocks; (5) the bypassing of main Arab urban centers; (6) the connection of Arab settlements to the road network.[3]

The short-term (1983–1986) development plan creates an order of priority for road construction that is based on the following criteria: "development of demand potential through road accessibility" (priority is measured by the number of planned Jewish housing units); "interconnecting regions of high Jewish settlement priority"; "circumventing Arab areas, opening up of new settlement areas."[4]

The road network (see maps 2 and 6) clearly reflects the aforementioned criteria. The emphasis falls on access roads from the new suburbs north of the trans-Samaria highway to the Tel Aviv conurbation and the interconnection of the Jerusalem metropolitan area. The plan also improves the direct connections (sometimes by creating new short links between existing roads) between the settlement regions in the east, west, and north of the West Bank. Clear efforts to bypass all large Arab towns are apparent. The map shows the Nablus, Qalqiliya, Tul Karm, and Jenin bypasses as well as shorter bypasses of Arab villages.

The existing and proposed road network clearly reflects Israeli partisan planning.[5] All roads are meant to serve Israel's local, regional, and national interests, while Arab transportation needs are ignored or are served as a byproduct of Israeli interests. In fact, the new West Bank road system can be defined as a dual system. There are new "Jewish roads," serving Jewish settlements and regions, and "Arab roads," the old pre-1967 network that will continue to serve Arab towns and villages. The interaction between the two networks is intentionally kept to a minimum. Israeli roads are planned to restrict Arab spatial sprawl. Road alignments 100 meters wide (in some places 150 meters wide; see proposed building line on map 3) are planned on the outskirts of Arab towns and villages to restrict their expansion and to prevent ribbon development along the roads. The Arabs, however, must pay for these roads. The tens of thousands of dunams needed for the new road network have been expropriated from Arab owners for "public purposes" (see chapter 4).

Restricted Military Areas

Restricted military areas cover 1.11 million dunams, or 53 percent of the total area seized for Israeli purposes in the West Bank. Map 4 and the figure of 1.11 million dunams define only the area that is officially declared, publicly announced, and actually used for military purposes. Large areas "closed for military purposes" or seized by the army have actually been given to settlements and other Jewish civilian uses. I therefore do not consider these areas military land use. Considerable areas of military camps, depots, and other military land uses are, of course, not marked on the map. To understand the placement of restricted military areas, I shall describe Israeli deployment strategies and the development of a military presence in the West Bank.[6]

Current Deployment of the Israel Defense Forces. The deployment of the Israel Defense Forces (IDF) on the West Bank is tailored to meet the threat of war on the Jordanian front and also to meet the problems of day-to-day security and to exploit the possibilities for other military land uses, such as training.

The operational and intelligence data upon which the IDF bases its considerations are classified. A substitute for official data can, however, be found in the monograph of Brigadier General Arieh Shalev, a retired senior officer of the IDF who, during the decade following 1967, served as the officer responsible for intelligence evaluation in the IDF and, later, as a regional commander on the West Bank. According to Shalev, the geographical and topographical givens of the West Bank and the relations of power between the IDF and the Arab armies on the Jordanian front together constitute the potential geostrategic threat facing Israel on that front. He notes:

> Against an enemy with offensive capabilities, Israel lacks sufficient strategic depth to defend the Coastal Plain, because Judea and Samaria are much higher and overlook the Coastal Plain. The width of the State of Israel in those regions is between 14 and 20 kilometers. According to Soviet estimates, that is the depth of a defensive division, and, according to the American estimate it is of a brigade. . . . Thus the defense of that area so vital to Israel from within the Green Line—strategic defense, taking everything into account—is possible merely on a tactical level because of the narrowness of the area. If the military threat against Israel persists, it is very doubtful whether it would be possible, over a long period of time, to succeed in the task of defending that vital area, where 67% of the inhabitants of Israel live, and to prevent a high number of losses, unless the depth is increased and the potential threat is removed to the other side of the Jordan. Moreover, an enemy that knows that in a single tactical maneuver he might be able to achieve the strategic goal of dividing Israel in its vital territory and perhaps even occupying parts of that territory, would be strongly tempted to try it. That knowledge alone would be enough to make the beginning of a war more likely.[7]

In the balance of the forces that, according to Shalev's estimate, pose a strategic danger to Israel, the IDF reckons four armies on the Eastern Front (Jordan, Syria, Iraq, and Saudi Arabia—and, according to some scenarios, Iran as well). Despite its name, the Eastern Front is in fact a geographical area containing a significant potential for military alliances. At present the aforementioned armies do not have a combined command, unified military doctrine, or significant experience in combined operations, but they do maintain connections (in recent years especially between Jordan and Iraq). If a political decision were made, the Jordanian government could offer the area from which to launch the war, and the main burden of forces could be supplied by Iraq and Syria.

Shalev emphasizes that although the Jordanian army in 1967 had only a defensive capacity against Israel, today it has the ability to wage a fast and mobile war and commands an advanced air force and surface-to-air defenses. Its battalions are mechanized and armored, unlike its infantry in the past, and it is mainly deployed in the triangle between the Sea of Galilee, the Dead Sea, and Zarka-Mafraq, close to its

emergency stations. The Jordanian deployment allows it to move westward to launch an attack without significant changes. The numerical relation between the standing armies, according to Shalev's monograph, gives clear superiority to the Arab land forces until all Israeli reserves have been called up:

> If a surprise attack by Jordan and Syria should occur, and at the same time an Iraqi expeditionary force began moving westward (without a clear picture of the behavior to be expected from Egypt), the IDF could place only two regular brigades against four to five Jordanian divisions and seven to eight Syrian ones. Therefore Syria and Jordan would have a numerical advantage of some six to one for at least the first forty-eight hours of the war, with respect to regular land forces. That is a quantitative advantage which the Arabs could exploit, making gains on the ground.[8]

The Central Command of the IDF is supposedly prepared for limited Jordanian actions as well, the success of which would be measured in local gains, "actions such as seizing territory close to the cease-fire lines, which would hurt Israel and arouse international reverberations."[9] According to that scenario, ever since Israel was deterred from accepting the American proposal of the Jericho Plan in 1974, which would have entailed voluntary withdrawal from an area in the Jordan Valley so that Jordan could claim some political success—the possibility has existed that Jordan might attempt to capture Jericho or to achieve a similar objective such that even military defeat might provide leverage for setting a dormant political process back in motion. The size of the regular forces that must be deployed by the IDF in the West Bank to delay an attack, according to those scenarios, while reserve forces are mobilized and the war is waged eastward of the Green Line (in addition to the observation stations manned by the intelligence corps, air radar stations, and ground-to-air missile batteries) is two armored or mobile brigades. That force is equal to a reduced division.

The History of Deployment. Immediately after the war in 1967, there were in fact two brigades on the West Bank, but the IDF did not choose to allocate an entire brigade to a quiet sector secondary in comparison to the Golan Heights and especially to Sinai and the Suez. Instead of a brigade or division, the IDF transferred training bases for the infantry, paramilitary units (Nahal), combat engineers, and basic training to the West Bank. It is customary, as a stage in the creation of facts, to attribute the idea of transferring the training bases to the West Bank to Ariel Sharon, the man who then served the General Staff in command of the training division.

According to Yitzhak Rabin, however, who was in 1967 the chief of staff, Minister of Defense Moshe Dayan actually initiated that action as early as June 1967, a few days after the war, to allow reserve forces to be demobilized and to maintain day-to-day security in the West Bank by means of the training bases (which were part of the regular army). Evidence in support of Rabin's account can be found in the intention, which had already been expressed in 1966 and may even have been voiced before that time, to remove the training bases from densely populated areas on the coastal plain. The Officers' Training School was actually transferred from Petah Tikva (near Tel Aviv) to Mitzpe Ramon in the Negev. A "city of training bases" was supposed to be built around it. The economic recession of 1966–1967 affected the defense budget adversely, and the plan for a city of training bases was deferred. The conquest of the West Bank brought about a combination of new necessities and opportunities. The training bases that were transferred to the West Bank were placed in abandoned Jordanian army bases, not in new facilities, the erection of which would have reflected different considerations with regard to deployment.

The most active war zone of the IDF in the West Bank, against the PLO organizations between the summer of 1967 and Black September of 1970, was the Jordan Valley. This sector was organized militarily as an infantry brigade command to which armored forces were attached. The organizational arrangement remained in force for more than a decade, during which most of the activity (after the defeat of the Palestine Liberation Organization in September 1970 and June 1971 and its expulsion from Jordan) concentrated on preventing the penetration of guerrilla groups across the Jordan. Those penetrations were much less frequent than during the hot pursuits of 1968–1969.

The Israeli-Egyptian peace process brought about a change in the deployment of the IDF in the West Bank. The Camp David agreement stipulated that after the establishment of autonomy in the West Bank, Israel could redeploy its forces in "defined security areas." The size of those areas and the extent of the forces stationed there were to be determined during the autonomy negotiations. In the General Staff of the IDF, some individuals feared that the bargaining would result in a freeze of the existing state of military deployment and would perhaps even determine a limited deployment. Raphael Eitan, who opposed any Israeli withdrawal from the West Bank and was at that time chief of staff, ordered the immediate expan-

sion of the areas designated for IDF training in the West Bank. Ezer Weizman, then minister of defense, subsequently said that according to Major General Eitan's interpretation, autonomy would be no more than "one autonomous Arab riding on a donkey between fire zones."[10]

Although the peace treaty between Israel and Egypt was not signed until March 1979 and the withdrawal from Sinai was carried out in two stages, being completed only in April 1982, Moshe Levi, who was then chief of Central Command (and afterwards chief of staff), realized that all IDF forces would be removed from Sinai and that they had to find new locations. The construction of the three new air bases in the Negev as replacements for the Etzion, Eitam, and Ofira bases in Sinai greatly reduced the deployment area of land-based forces in the Negev. The transfer of the main thrust of the military threat from the southwest to the northeast also assisted Levi in convincing the chief of staff that it would be better to transfer some of the regular army that had previously been based in Sinai to the area of the Central Command, that is, the West Bank. The new deployment took the form of a logistical infrastructure (camps, installations, emergency supply depots) and a more thorough use of training areas.

It should be added that the shortage of training areas within Israel has been cited as an additional reason for not withdrawing the IDF from the West Bank. The claim has been made that since the strengthening of the IDF from 1967 onward (the addition of thousands of tanks, other military equipment, and about ten additional divisions), it has no longer been possible to return to the other side of the pre-June 1967 borders. This contention is not, however, accepted by all military experts. An alternative view is that it is possible to use the training areas more efficiently and to improve the location of the various bases and that the solution to various political problems should not be made dependent on the apparent constraint of the need for training areas for the IDF.

Most restricted military areas do not compete with other land uses, except grazing, although Arab cultivation in some patches has had to be abandoned in the eastern strip. With the improvement of security conditions on the bank of the River Jordan, about 80,000 dunams beyond the security fence were released by the military and were handed over to Jewish settlers. On the western part of the West Bank, considerable areas used for military purposes (because of proximity to the armistice line) were not released after 1967. Some of these areas are suitable for other land uses. Some Jordanian army camps and military areas taken over by the IDF after 1967 were handed over for Israeli civilian land uses.

Nature Reserves and Parks

Nature reserves and parks appear in table 7 as Jewish-controlled areas. These land uses seem to be "neutral" and should therefore be treated as an amenity for the benefit of all inhabitants, irrespective of ethnic affiliation. This view, however, is unfortunately not shared by Israeli "competent authorities." The declarations of nature reserve areas, covering 250,000 dunams by 1983 and, in the final stage, 340,000 dunams, are part of the program of "land seizure." According to WZO *Plan, 1983–1986,* "afforestation, grazing areas and parks" are part of a "program for land seizure prepared by a decision of the Ministerial Committee for Settlement . . . dated 26.7.81." The nature reserve areas are part of a larger plan for the creation of archaeological and historical parks. "Land seizure by creating parks" is aimed at "the prevention of unsuitable development" (apparently by Arabs) but is meant at the same time to "keep open the option of developing tourist enterprises at a later stage," thus "creating employment for the [Jewish] settlers." According to the official plan, "*in addition* to the benefit of seizing land *other* benefits can be accrued, such as monetary profits, improvement of the quality of life *and* the environment, etc."[11]

Although the declaration of nature reserve areas does not expropriate the land, it severely restricts all other land uses and practically forbids all development. It should be noted that although new areas were declared as nature reserves, British Mandatory nature and forest reserves have been partially reclassified as development areas for Jewish settlements (the Umm-Reihan and Umm-Safa forest reserves). Nature reserve land use therefore must be treated as an integral part of the Israeli land control system. Because of conflicting information, nature reserve areas have been counted in table 7 as part of the general area of "state land." At least some of the declared park lands are outside areas designated as state land and therefore should be added to the 2,150,000 dunams thus defined (they are discussed in the section "Land Seized by Declaring It 'State Land'").

Land Use Planning

The Military Government. Official land use planning and licensing procedures have been a major instrument in Israeli efforts to gain control over space in the territories. The military government was aware of the enormous political importance of land use planning, but during the first years of occupation the volume of building starts and the need to secure land for Jewish settlement were small. Planning and licensing remained chaotic. Except in the Jordan Valley area and

where military purposes were concerned, the issue of land use planning remained secondary. In 1970, when building activity picked up, the military government issued Order 393 on building inspection. The order empowered a military commander to forbid construction, to stop it, or to impose conditions on it. Later the military government sought to regulate the planning process in a more orderly fashion. Therefore Order 418 was issued in March 1971. It amended the Jordanian town and village planning law passed in 1966. Under the new order, the structure of the traditional hierarchical planning committees (local, district, and national) as it existed under the British and as it had been maintained in Israel and the West Bank and the customary composition of the planning committees (government, institutional, and local membership) were abolished. Instead, all planning powers were vested in the Higher Planning Committee, appointed by the military commander and composed of Israeli officials only.

District planning committees were abolished, and independent planning powers of villages were vested in a Village Planning Committee, appointed also by the military commander. Even licensing powers of the municipalities were restricted. The Higher Planning Committee was empowered to amend, cancel, or suspend any plan or license, to assume all powers vested in any local committee, and to exempt any person from the need to obtain a planning license. Involvement of West Bank inhabitants in the land use planning process became minimal. Although there was some reorganization of the central planning office (serving the Higher Planning Committee), the planning process, and especially enforcement, remained erratic. In the mid-1970s, for example, the single planner responsible for the professional work of the Higher Planning Committee was employed only part time. The number of reported building violations in 1972–1973 was sixty-two, although the number of unlicensed buildings reached thousands.

Until 1977 the main effort of the military government in controlling land use planning was to safeguard Israeli interest in the Allon Plan areas (the Jordan Valley and the Etzion block), which were virtually uninhabited by Arabs, and to keep spaces open around military installations and strategic roads. There was little effort to restrict Arab building or to curb sprawl outside the built-up Arab areas. The result of this policy is manifest from the preceding discussion of Arab built-up areas.

Israeli Planning. In 1977 the Likud government, following its policy of "settlement in all parts of Eretz Israel," entirely changed its West Bank land use planning strategy. Instead of limiting its interest to the

Allon Plan areas, it emphasized comprehensive re-gionwide land use planning and enforcement. In-stead of spot planning that allowed Arab sprawl, the Likud planners sought to achieve firm Israeli control over the entire West Bank and severely to restrict Arab construction outside the nuclear towns and villages.

The planning process was expanded and strengthened. Planning decisions on parks, roads, Jewish settlement areas, and other land uses have been brought regularly to the Ministerial Committee on Settlements; high-level coordinating committees composed of representatives of the ministries of Agri-culture, Defense, Interior, and Housing and the WZO have been assisted by professional multidisciplinary planning teams. The Higher Planning Committee be-came the legal instrument for action by these land use planning bodies. With the creation of the Jewish re-gional councils (see chapter 5), their areas of jurisdic-tion were declared "special planning regions." The Jewish councils became "special planning commis-sions" with powers equal to those of the Arab munici-palities. A "district committee" was instituted, but only for the Jewish areas. An impressive body of stud-ies and plans has been compiled, and through them trends in land use planning of the West Bank can be monitored. The plans, on the level of "master plans," are explicitly sectarian. The planning principles are political directives expressed in professional planning jargon. The criteria established to determine priorities of settlement regions are "*interconnection* [havirah] be-tween existing Jewish areas for the creation of [Jewish] settlement continuity" and "*separation* [hayitz] to re-strict uncontrolled Arab settlement and the preven-tion of Arab settlement blocs"; "*scarcity* [hesekh] re-fers to areas devoid of Jewish settlement." In these criteria "pure planning and political planning ele-ments are included."[12]

A quantitative point system was introduced to identify priority areas. The result is described on map 5. The high-priority areas encompass the central mas-sif of the West Bank in such a way as to encircle the populated Arab areas. In the words of the plan: "In this strip (along the watershed from North-Samaria to South-Judea) most of the Arab population is concen-trated in urban and rural settlements. The watershed highway is in essence a *local Arab road* axis. Jewish settlement along this axis will create a mental [sic] separation, in relation to the mountain massif. Also, it [Jewish settlement] may restrict uncontrolled Arab building sprawl." The extension of the high-priority Jewish settlement area to the northwest of the West Bank as far as the armistice line is explained thus: "An area along the Green Line from Reihan to east of Tul Karm and east of Elkanah [is] liable [sic] to become an Arab settlement block, therefore separation through settlement activity and legislation [to restrict

Arab building] is necessary and imperative."[13] Arab populated areas are considered "problematic" for set-tlement because "the chances for land acquisition are small, and there is continuous Arab settlement or in-tensive agricultural cultivation." Nevertheless, Jewish Settlement Plan 2010 (map 6) envisages the fragmen-tation of Arab settlement blocks as they appear on the 1983–1986 development plan (map 5).

Arab population and Arab land use are regarded as constraints. Arab areas are encircled in the first stage and are then penetrated and fragmented. The planners admit that the master plan and development plan did not venture to study seriously "the effect of Jewish settlement on Arab population." Nevertheless, they identified and isolated "positive and negative interactions." Negative interactions are the result of "unplanned and uncontrolled internal migration of the two populations." The uncontrolled Jewish inter-nal migration is not defined but is described as "pene-tration to Arab population centers," apparently a ref-erence to the Jewish attempts to settle in Nablus proper. The negative consequences of Arab migration are made explicit. They include "the creation of Arab shanty towns in Jewish population centers"; "the un-controlled expansion of townships and villages in the Jerusalem area and western Samaria which creates a separation with all that that implies between the new settlements and the existing ones"; "the creation of [new] centers of gravity [sic] and new 'foci' of influ-ence in the large Arab towns." Finally, it is said that "migration would adversely affect Arab society" in that emigrants would leave the "traditional social en-vironment [and move] to a new environment, that is generally more hostile [to Israel]."[14]

The planners propose to fight "negative conse-quences of Arab migration" by "restricting Arab com-muting and encouraging *homogeneous* growth of Arab settlements." The methods suggested include the drawing up of statutory land use plans for Arab settle-ments based on double the existing population; in-creased densities and the definition of specific land uses; the development of enforcement agencies to prevent violation of the new land use plans; the en-couragement of employment in the villages; restric-tions on the development of large Arab industrial zones in urban centers and their vicinity; and finally the "expansion of Jewish construction in the areas."[15] The Israeli planners do not pretend to use profes-sional, objective planning criteria. They are proud of their partisan approach. The declared plan objective is "*to disperse maximally large Jewish population* in areas of high settlement priority, using small national in-puts and in a relatively short period by using the set-tlement potential of the West Bank and to achieve the incorporation [of the West Bank] into the [Israeli] na-tional system."[16]

The plan bears the insignia of the State of Israel, however, and is based on the work of a team composed of representatives of (for example) the ministries of Defense, Interior, and Housing and specialized agencies such as the Land Authority, the Electrical Corporation, and Public Works as well as the military government, the civil administration, and the Higher Planning Committee. The plan is based on surveys and plans and quotes the ministerial committee's decision. It cannot be viewed as other than the official land use plan for the West Bank. That its "principles" are implemented by the West Bank Statutory Higher Planning Committee is shown by the new statutory outline scheme (1982) for a 275,000-dunam area bordering on Jerusalem (see map 3). The main principles of this scheme are simple: to check future expansion of Arab towns and villages. The planners assume double the present population of Arab settlements at increased densities; the open space is defined either as "special areas" (that is, areas already seized or defined as "state land"—designated implicitly for Jewish settlement) or as agricultural areas, nature reserves, or areas for future planning. The planners fixed extremely wide building lines on either side of arterial and secondary roads—that is, 100–150 meters—to check expansion of Arab settlements, to dissect them, and to prevent ribbon development.

Other statutory plans are being prepared by the Higher Planning Committee for Arab areas. The preamble of Order 418 (which vested all planning powers in the Higher Planning Committee) reads: "Whereas I consider it necessary for the orderly management of development and construction operations in the Area, and for securing proper planning and licensing procedures, I order. . . ." From the perspective of 30,000 Israeli settlers, "proper planning and licensing procedures" seem to have been carried out smoothly. From the perspective of 750,000 West Bank Palestinians, the preamble reads like a macabre joke.

Notes

1. One source for the data on Jewish built-up areas is *Military Orders 783, 982* as amended; maps attached to the document have dotted lines showing the boundaries of existing settlements. See also *Master Plan and Development Plan for Settlement in Samaria and Judaea* (Jerusalem: World Zionist Organization, Ministry of Agriculture, April 1983), sec. 1A,

tables 1A, 1B, 1C. In my text and notes I shall henceforth refer to this plan as WZO *Plan, 1983–1986*. Other sources were Ministry of Housing, *Settlement in Judea and Samaria: Activity and Planning*, prepared for the Knesset Economic Committee (Jerusalem, June 1983), maps; development plans of the regional councils for Shomron (1982), Matei Binyamin (May 1982), Etzion (August 1982), Jordan Valley (June 1982), and Har Hebron (July 1982); and the West Bank Data Base Project index of settlements.

2. The "sphere of influence" of Arab built-up areas was determined by charting areas with a housing pattern that indicates built-up character as appearing on a 1:50,000 ordinance survey map (Survey of Israel, State of Israel, Tel Aviv, 1982). See n. 1 in table 7, this volume; Arab municipalities, official boundaries as amended, municipal and planning boundaries; outline area plan change 1/82 to Area Plan RJ5; Ministry of the Interior, *Judea and Samaria—Guidelines for Physical Planning* (Jerusalem, 1971).

3. WZO *Plan, 1983–1986*, sec. 2.2.1.2.

4. Ibid., sec. 2.3.1.

5. Data on pre-1967 roads come from Shalom Reichman and Shmuel Sharir, *In Judea and Samaria: Essays in Settlement Geography*, vol. 1 (Jerusalem: Kna'an, 1972), pp. 117–24 (including bibliography). Data on post-1967 roads come from Ordinance Survey maps: WZO *Plan, 1983–1986*, map 3; roads development plan 1986. Roads marked as existing include roads under construction and right of way secured by land expropriation until August 1983. Planned roads are marked roads that in my opinion are seriously planned. See also WZO *Plan, 1983–1986*, sec. 2.2.1, p. 27, and tables; Ministry of Housing, *Settlement in Judea and Samaria*; World Zionist Organization, *Plan of Hundred Thousand Settlers* (Jerusalem, 1982). On road development, see the development plans of the regional councils cited in n.1.

6. Sources for data on restricted military areas are Arieh Shalev, *The West Bank: Line of Defense* (Tel Aviv: Hakibutz Hamenchad, 1982), text and maps; Survey of Israel, State of Israel, Tel Aviv, Ordinance Survey maps prepared for the Nature Reserve Association, 1982 (areas defined on the maps in the legend as "Area Restricted for Hiking [training area]").

7. Shalev, *The West Bank*, p.38.

8. Ibid., p. 54.

9. Ibid., p. 128.

10. Quoted to author by a journalist, Amir Oren.

11. WZO *Plan, 1983–1986*, secs. 5.2.2, 5.2.5.1, 5.2.2. Emphasis added in this and the following quotations. Data on nature reserve areas came from Survey of Israel 1.100,000 (areas defined in map legends as "nature reserves").

12. WZO *Plan, 1983–1986*, sec. 2.1.3.

13. Ibid., sec. 2.1.4.2.

14. Ibid., sec. 2.7.

15. Ibid.

16. Ibid., sec. 1.1.

Appendix

In addition to the other sources, the sources for land areas for industry, agriculture, and grazing that appear in table 7 are the following: *Industry—WZO Plan, 1983–1986*, sec. 2.4, p. 37, and 4.6, p. 105; WZO, *Plan of Hundred Thousand Settlers. Agriculture—Jewish*: Regional council planning directives for Jordan Valley, Matei Binyamin, and Etzion, text, tables, and maps; Kahan, "Agriculture and Water in the West Bank and Gaza," part 2; *Arab*: Ordinance Survey map 1:50,000 (Survey of Israel, 1982), information on plantations (olives, vineyards, citrus orchards); Kahan, "Agriculture and Water," part 1, especially pp. 20–24. *Grazing, fallow, marginally cultivable*: *Jewish*: WZO *Plan, 1983–1986*, sec. 5.2.4, p. 123; *Arab*: Kahan, "Agriculture and Water," pp. 20–24.

Sources for total land use—Jewish: Areas defined as "state land" in all categories (except road expropriation) were computed by adding up all areas marked on map 7, which was charted according to Military Orders 783, 982 showing jurisdictional boundaries of regional and local councils. Interpretation of these areas as "state land" is based on the Matei Binyamin regional council planning directives, sec. 4.1.C: "the jurisdictional area of Matei Binyamin is a collection of areas on a map attached to the administrative order concerning regional councils [order 982]. *These areas are in fact delineated according to the Land Authority survey ('purple maps'), and also areas of seizure orders, expropriation orders and state land declarations."* Land Authority "purple maps" are confidential. According to the Etzion planning directives, sec. C.4.1, p. 22, "In 1978 a survey was conducted by the Land Authority whose objective was to identify *all uncultivated* lands in the West Bank, under the assumption that [these lands] will be declared [as state lands] or will be seized. This survey is today being updated and completed." On the legal procedure, see above.

The total figure of 2,150,000 dunams is independently corroborated by WZO *Plan 1983–1986*, p. 16, and also by Pliah Albek in a statement to the press (see chap. 4, this volume, n. 9). The survey of uncultivated and unregistered land might claim, in addition to the above areas, also part of the grazing and fallow areas (1,675,000 dunams) and 'miri' cultivated lands.

Sources for total land use—Arab: Total defined land use areas as arrived at by adding up all the figures in the relevant columns in table 7 related to Arab land use.

4

The Scramble for Space: Land Ownership

Issues concerning land ownership in the West Bank and Gaza are mainly perceived in their sectarian context. Intraethnic civil, commercial, and legal land ownership matters are overshadowed by the macronational struggle for control of space. It is impossible to describe land ownership in the occupied territories in the professional jargon of title deeds, land registration, and settlement claims. It is also impossible to describe a stable and consistent legal framework governing land ownership. The Israeli authorities, in their quest to take possession of land in the territories, have been using every legal and quasi-legal means in the book and are inventing new ones to attain their objectives.

A variety of definitions and classifications have been used to determine "land under direct Israeli possession," and controversies abound on the true meaning of measures taken by the Israelis concerning land ownership—whether "requisition," "expropriation," "closure," "declaration of state land," and "absentee property" constitute outright and absolute seizure or just requisition for the duration. Some observers view land use restrictions as land seizure, compounding the confusion. The controversy is reflected in the conflicting estimates of the size of the expropriated area, which varies between a quarter and two-thirds of the total area of the West Bank.

In the following discussion "area in direct Israeli possession" is defined as an area over which an owner or a holder cannot exercise rights of ownership or possession because of legal, quasi-legal, or coercive measures undertaken by the military government or other official and quasi-official Israeli agencies. More simply, these are areas taken from the Palestinian community and given over to Israeli use, whether official, communal, or private, or to further sectarian Israeli interests. It should be observed that land use restrictions do not fall under this definition, because

ownership rights, though curtailed, are not affected. Land requisitioned without change of ownership, however, and "closed areas" used for military purposes do fall under the definition, because a barrier has been created between the owners and their land.

The various Israeli methods of sequestering land that fall within the definition are listed and described in turn.

Absentee Property

Land and other property owned by citizens of the West Bank who left the area in 1967 or before were vested by Order 58 (1967) in the custodian of abandoned property. The custodian was empowered to manage the property and to lease it. The total area thus seized amounts to 430,000 dunams and 11,000 structures.[1] The majority of the area was "leased" to relatives of the absentees or was given to them to "manage" and therefore cannot be considered under Israeli possession. The custodian also leased about 25,000–30,000 dunams, however, to Israeli agricultural settlements, mainly in the Jordan Valley.

Registered State Land

Land registered in the name of the Jordanian government as "state land" according to Jordanian laws (legislation passed in 1963 and 1965) should not be confused with "declared state land," which I discuss below. The military government took possession of that land by virtue of Order 59 (1967), which also established the Administration of Government Property. The administration was empowered to execute all transactions concerning the administration of the property. The area of registered state land is estimated at 750,000 dunams.

Land Requisitioned for Military Purposes

Privately owned land seized by the military government under an order proclaiming that the area is "required for essential and urgent military needs" remains theoretically under private ownership, and the military government offers payment for the "use" of the land. The legal basis quoted by the Israelis is article 52 of the Hague regulations, which reads: "Requisition in kind and services shall not be demanded from local authorities or inhabitants *except for the need of the army of occupation.*" Requisition "for military purposes" had been the method used until 1980 to secure land for Israeli settlements. The High Court of Justice accepted Israeli military statements that "all Israeli settlements in the administered territories are an integral part of the Territorial Defense System of the IDF" and ruled that the continued use of such areas by civilian settlement constitutes, indeed, "urgent military needs." A question arose: How can a permanent settlement be established on an area temporarily requisitioned? The High Court of Justice accepted the attorney general's answer that

> the civilian settlement [in question] can only exist in that place as long as the army occupies the area by virtue of the Requisition Order. This occupation can itself come to an end some day as a result of international negotiations leading to a new arrangement which will take effect under international law and determine the face of the settlement as of other settlements existing in the Administered Territories.[2]

The total area thus requisitioned is estimated at 35,000 dunams.

The requisition method of securing land for Jewish settlements, however, became obsolete after the accession to power of the Likud government. The modest, security-oriented settlement policy of Labor governments could make use of military-related requisitions. The Likud refused to hide behind military excuses. It publicly announced that it is "the right of the Jewish people to settle in Judea and Samaria." "Not immediate and urgent military needs" but "national security needs in the broad sense" were the reason for land requisition. The new policy of massive settlement and the building of urban centers in all parts of the West Bank required more ambitious methods of land acquisitions.[3]

When the new settlement of Elon Moreh was established in 1979 on land requisitioned for "military needs," the Likud government did not take the position that "the settlement can exist only as long as the army occupies the area." Ideological imperatives compelled the officials to declare in the High Court that they regard the Elon Moreh settlement as a permanent Jewish settlement no less than Degania (the seventy-year-old first kibbutz) or Netanya (a coastal town). The High Court of Justice ruled that "article 52 cannot include on any reasonable interpretation, national security needs in the broad sense." It ordered that the requisition be rescinded, because "the decision to establish a permanent settlement destined from the outset to remain in its place indefinitely . . . comes up against insurmountable legal obstacles, because no military government can create facts in its area for its military needs which are designated 'ab initio' to persist even after the end of the military rule in that area, when the fate of the area after the termination of military rule is still unknown."[4] The government decided to abandon that method, but not before an easier and more efficient method had been devised (see the section "Land Seized by Declaring It 'State Land'").

Land Closed for Training Purposes

The military government declares from time to time "the closure of training areas" by virtue of clause 2(2), 70 of Military Order 3 (1967). Training areas are demarcated on maps that are open "for inspection by all concerned." The total area thus closed is estimated at 1.15 million dunams. In some cases the military allows cultivation when the area is not used by it for training grounds, firing ranges, and so on. In some cases, however, closure of an area is a prelude to requisition. The Kiryat Arba and Beqa'ot areas, for example, were initially closed areas and were later transformed into "requisitioned" areas—for Jewish settlements. Closed areas used by Jewish settlements are estimated at about 5,000 dunams.

Jewish Land

Land owned by Jews before 1948 and administered by the Jordanian custodian of enemy property is estimated at 30,000 dunams, most located in the Jerusalem metropolitan area and the Etzion Block.

Land Expropriated for Public Purposes

The "compulsory purchase" of land is based on the Jordanian law "Expropriation of Land for Public Purposes" (No. 2, 1953). The military government amended this law (Orders 131, 321, 949) to facilitate wholesale expropriations with minimal checks and balances. Since the law specifies clearly, however, that expropriation can be carried out only for the benefit of the public, the military government could not use it for taking land and handing it over to Israeli settlers (as the Israeli government can do under the Mandatory Ordinance of 1943 still in force in Israel). The military government, however, has made extensive use of the amended Jordanian laws for acquiring land for roads to Israeli settlements and for installations such as water reservoirs and cesspools.

Land Seized by Declaring It "State Land"

By 1976 Israeli land experts completed the survey of absentee and government properties and took possession of these categories of land by virtue of Orders 58 and 59. These areas, however, though extensive, could not provide a firm base for massive Israeli settlements, as envisaged by the new Likud government. The lands are scattered, and most registered state land is located in areas unsuitable for settlement. When the method of requisition for military purposes became obsolete in 1979, the pressure to devise new methods mounted. The need for a new policy also came as a result of the signing of the peace treaty with Egypt and the impending autonomy talks. The issue of control of state land became one of the most controversial in the negotiations on the powers and responsibilities of the self-governing authority (see chapter 5).

Israeli experts who dealt with Israeli-Arab land matters offered a solution. They suggested that the criteria that applied in Israel proper vis-à-vis the Arab population be implemented in the territories: instead of claiming land piecemeal, Israeli officials should turn the tables and view "all land as national patrimony, except what the [Arab] villages can prove is theirs under the narrowest interpretation of the law."[5] In 1978 a survey of West Bank land was carried out. It classified the area into nonarable (stony), arable but fallow, and cultivated lands. The assumption was that all uncultivated land in the West Bank would be seized if it was not registered.

It should be noted that two-thirds of the area of the West Bank has not yet gone through the legal process of settlement of land claims. By this process owners are given the chance to declare that they possess land and to prove their title to it. They can then register the land in their names in the Land Registry and can thus secure indisputable title to it. In the Hebron and Bethlehem subdistricts (except the towns), half the Ramallah subdistrict, the southern part of the Nablus subdistrict, and the majority of the Tul Karm subdistrict, the process either had not begun by 1967 or had not been completed. In 1968 Order 291, "concerning water and land settlement," suspended all settlement orders. It temporarily halted all proceedings in the settlement of land claims. Since 1968 the proceedings have not been renewed, even in cases that were near completion. According to Israeli sources, the reason given for freezing land settlement

proceedings in the region was that the military government "did not wish to prejudice the rights of the inhabitants of the Hashemite Kingdom east of the River Jordan or of absentee landlords."[6] It should be mentioned that "absentee landlords" are not permitted to enter the West Bank, even for a visit, lest they claim land on which Jewish settlements have been established. According to the same Israeli source, the suspension of the settlement of land claims "does not in any way prejudice any existing rights in such land."[7] Internal directives of the Land Authority, however, state specifically that "if the area is not registered and land claims settled, one can assume that the area can be claimed as state land, if the land is not cultivated." The directives set the procedure by which state land can be located:

> One should distinguish between cultivated and built-up land—and stony fields. Cultivated land can be claimed by the owners by virtue of the Law of Possession. The owner, however, must be assisted in his claim by the testimony of the Mukhtar [village elder] and others, that he has cultivated his land continuously. Then he must submit *Maliyyh* [a proof of Land Tax payment]. It is customary to view stony fields or *"Ard al-Mawat"* as Jordanian state land and therefore the State of Israel is now the custodian over that land. Stony fields situated within a radius of 1.8 kilometers from the center of a village belong to that village.[8]

The area thus located and charted amounts (with other forms of requisition) to 2.15 million dunams and is demarcated on map 7. A comparison of Arab agriculture (shown in map 8) with the state land map shows clearly that most areas designated for seizure are uncultivated. In May 1980 the Israeli cabinet accepted in principle the new criterion for "state land," and a special ministerial committee immediately implemented the decision, sanctioning the expansion of the areas of six settlements. A special assistant attorney general was appointed to inspect and verify each application by the Land Authority (formally the administrator of government property), as specified by Order 58, to declare an area state domain. In a statement to the press, Pliah Albek, then special assistant, said that "the land does not include tracts which have been cultivated during the past 10 years or land registered as privately owned."[9]

The decision of the Israeli cabinet on state land should be regarded as a major step toward the annexation of the West Bank. Not only was 40 percent of its total area thus taken from the Palestinians and put at the disposal of Israelis for unlimited settlements, but the last pretense of maintaining the temporary nature of land seizure arrangements was dropped. The old devices of military acquisition and closure "for the duration" were replaced by a new concept identifying government property in the West Bank and Gaza as Israeli national patrimony. Land policies in the territories and in Israel have become identical. In both areas

> National Patrimony has consistently been taken to mean only the Jewish population. Land settlements and development on areas adjudicated to the state in all of its capacities—vacant land, public land, state domain, Arab Absentee Property, etc.—have been assigned exclusively to Jewish institutions, settlements and individuals. . . . New Legislation, administrative regulations, and executive policies and procedures have been fo-
> :ting or altering the legal
> illagers could claim land
> n land already held by

> abled the Israeli authorities
> hat no Arab land had been
> government was acting in
> and international law. The
> I that the administrator of
> acting within his legal
> state land, that the new
> ion of Jordanian law, and
> in Order 58 enabled the
> ly with its obligation un-
> onvention. A petition of
> to the High Court was
> only 4 dunams of 7,000
> I were registered under
> easury. No other peti-
> ge the legality of claim-
> ehalf of the Jordanian
> it for a forty-nine-year
> ban development. No-
> ation of how that act
> ling that the military
> "designed 'ab initio'
> military rule in the

rk used by Israel to and Gaza land as national patrimony is based on a medieval law of conquest and on Moslem principle, both embodied in an Ottoman law dated 1858 that applies on the West Bank and Gaza. Conquerors in the Middle Ages regarded themselves as the owners of all lands that came under their control. The seigneur, suzerain, or sultan retained ultimate ownership of the land while distributing it to his vassals, who held the fiefs under feudal law. Only two categories were held under different tenure al-

most independently of the feudal system: land held by a church or monastery (in Europe) or by the *Waqf* (Moslem charitable trust) and land held by town tenure (*burgage* in Europe or *mulk* in the Ottoman Empire). When the feudal system became defunct in the Ottoman Empire and was legally abolished in 1839, the fief holders were replaced by tax collectors. To regularize taxation on land tenure, a land code was promulgated in 1858. The code distinguishes between two categories of real property: The first consisted of *Waqf* properties, administered under Moslem sharia courts, and *mulk*, generally town property held under valid title deeds. The second category consisted of land that the sultan ultimately owned by virtue of the law of conquest. This category is divided into three classes:

> 1) *Miri* is cultivable land to which holders could claim possession if they continuously cultivated it. Theoretically, if the land remained fallow for three years, a holder could lose his or her rights, and the land would then become known as *mahlul* (severed).
> 2) *Matrouk* is land for public use, such as roads, commons, and pasture.
> 3) *Mawat* is wasteland defined in article 103 of the code thus:

> Vacant land which is not in possession of anyone by title deed [*tapu*] or assigned "ab antiquo" to the use of inhabitants of a town or village and lies at such a distance from towns and villages from which a human voice cannot be heard at the nearest inhabited place. [Land] such as: rocky mountains [*tashlik*], wild fields [*otalik*] and bushland [*franlik*] is called Mawat [dead] land. Anyone who is in need may cultivate it, as sown land gratuitously, with the leave of the official, on the condition that the ultimate ownership [*raqabah*] shall belong to the sultan and that all the laws concerning cultivated lands shall apply to this [newly cultivated] land.[12]

Under the British, a new category of state land was introduced, and a process of settlement of land claims began. The Ottoman land code remained in force, however, with only minor amendments. The Jordanians for their part also kept the Turkish system, with some alterations. Neither the British nor the Jordanians claimed, declared, or registered *miri*, *matrouk*, or *mawat* land as state land by virtue of a hypothetical sultan's ultimate right of ownership; but if as a result of a process of settlement of land claims there remained tracts not claimed by anyone, these tracts were registered as state lands. Members of the rural community were not interested in registering barren, remote, and nonarable tracts on which they would be liable to pay taxes. The settlement officers, who had to define every plot, cited these unclaimed tracts as *muattallah* (land out of use) and registered it in the name of the high commissioner in trust for the government of Palestine during the mandate or under the Jordanian Treasury after 1948. The Israeli military government took possession of all state land registered as a result of the completion of the process of settlement of claims. As previously mentioned, the process has been completed in only one-third of the West Bank area, and in 1968 the military government suspended the process for the remaining area.

In 1980 the Israelis introduced a new principle: *By virtue of the sultan's ultimate* (but theoretical) *ownership, all unregistered and uncultivated land is claimed as state land*. The internal Israeli directives are the practical application of this principle, and its connection with the Ottoman land code and especially with article 103 is clear.

Purporting to safeguard property that an ousted sovereign never claimed, the military government, which otherwise does not recognize the legitimacy of the Jordanian regime in the West Bank, claims that it is complying with the civilized principles of a belligerent occupation. In fact, the government evokes a medieval law of conquest. William of Tyre, the chronicler of the Crusades (1130–1184), describes the medieval process. The crusaders

> had agreed that after it had been taken by force, whatever each man might win for himself should be his forever by right of possession without molestation . . . they penetrated into the most retired and out-of-the-way places and broke open the most private apartments of the foe. At the entrance of each house, as it was taken, the victor hung up his shield and his arms as a sign to all who approached not to pause there but to pass by that place as already in possession of another.[13]

The Israeli process of declaration and seizure is not the outcome of a long, multistage judicial process but was intended specifically to preempt it. The administrator of government property issues an order declaring certain tracts state land. The declaration is final; the administrator does not have to show cause for the decision. The only legal remedy open to the affected citizen is to appeal to an appeal committee within twenty-one days. The appeal committees, constituted under Order 172 (1967), are composed solely of regular Israeli officers or reserve officers. Each committee decides on its own procedure and is not bound by the rules of evidence or procedures except by the right of the appellant to appear before it and to submit

his or her claims and evidence. Proceedings may be held in camera, and the decisions are not subject to appeal. The appeal committee is empowered to recommend that the military commander cancel an action, amend it, or take any other action. If the recommendation is not accepted or if the committee did not recommend any of these three courses, the decision that was the subject of the appeal remains in force (Order 172 [6]). The landowner who has the status of an appellant bears the onus of proving his or her case. Landowners, most of whom are villagers, must produce documents, maps, and measurements that they do not possess. Although according to "internal directives" the committees may accept receipts of payment of land tax, many villagers in the past evaded payment because the land had been marginally cultivated, and they are therefore unable to produce receipts. Because the area is "unsettled," the only irrefutable document of ownership, a title deed, cannot be produced. Confronting the villagers stands a battery of government legal experts and surveyors equipped with maps, aerial photos, and ancient Ottoman documents discovered by special teams in the Istanbul archives. The appeal committee is frequently headed by a senior legal adviser of the Israel Land Authority. It is therefore not surprising that Arab inhabitants lose most appeals.

It should be noted that the ultimate test of possession in unregistered areas relates to cultivation. Therefore the Israeli authorities have an interest in restricting or even forbidding cultivation so that the land can be claimed as *mawat* or *mahlul*. Order 1015 (1983) forbids, under penalty of imprisonment, the planting of fruit trees without permission and prior submission of documents of ownership. Order 1039 (1983) extended the prohibition to vegetable cultivation. Israeli authorities consider grazing and cultivation, even on areas that have only been earmarked for state land and have not yet been declared as such, to be trespassing. Israeli settler "patrols" seize sheep and arrest farmers in these areas in order to prevent "illegal trespass."

The ancient principle of ownership limited by use was introduced by the medieval conquerors to encourage cultivation and thus to increase their dues on the yields. The Israeli conqueror is not interested in revenues but in vacant land on which to settle his own people. Therefore the authorities define Arab cultivation as invasion (*plisha*) and have created an elaborate system to "guard the land." The responsibility for guarding the land has been entrusted to the Jewish National Fund (JNF). The veteran Zionist agency responsible for land purchase in the prestate period and for land reclamation thereafter is now in charge of carrying out a plan for land seizure. Its objectives are to "safeguard the boundaries of areas seized for Jewish settlements." The JNF "safeguards" the seized areas through afforestation, grazing, and parks. The total budget for afforestation of 31,900 dunams is estimated at $6.82 million. The total area planned for grazing is 140,000 dunams. The cost is estimated at $5.6 million.[14]

By 1983 the total area for which the declaration of state land process has been completed and of which the authorities have taken actual possession amounted to 400,000 dunams, or 25 percent of the total area earmarked.[15] The authorities continue the process according to the requests of the settlement agencies. Evidence of land ownership that the appeal committees deem inadequate to contest state land declaration becomes valid when it involves Jewish land purchase. When local Arab courts "interfered" in such transactions by issuing court injunctions based on evidence of false documents, the military government (Order 1060 of 1983) "removed all matters concerning land on which a request for registration had been submitted" from the local (that is, Arab) courts, and vested them in a special committee (constituted in 1971). In the liberal days of 1971, however, that committee was chaired by an Arab judge. The military government has now removed the judge and has appointed the civil governor instead.

This is not the only measure introduced to facilitate Jewish purchase of land in the West Bank. In July 1967 the military government issued an order forbidding any land transaction without a written permit. The Israeli government at that time sought to channel all Jewish land purchase through the Jewish National Fund. In 1971 a general permit to "execute land transactions" was granted to Himanuta, a subsidiary of the JNF. In 1973 the Israel Land Authority submitted a "plan for land purchase" that specified the locations, purchase priorities, and procedures. In 1973 Moshe Dayan (then minister of defense) proposed that a general permit to purchase land be issued to private Israeli corporations and individuals. The Israeli cabinet turned down his proposal and decided that land purchase would remain nationalized. Between 1972 and 1977 some 12,000 dunams were purchased at a cost of 12 million Israeli pounds (about $1.7 million). Many transactions were not registered in the official Land Registry but were carried out by receiving an "irrevocable power of attorney" from the owner. Arab sellers preferred this confidential method to appearing publicly in the Land Registry office. The validity of the power of attorney, however, is limited by Jordanian law to five years. Since many transactions were questionable, the Israeli buyers delayed registration, and many irrevocable powers of attorney became void. Consequently, the military government issued Order 811 (1979), extending the validity of the purchase doc-

uments to ten years. A year later Order 847 extended the term to fifteen years.

In September 1979 the Israeli government lifted the ban on private Jewish land purchase, and a rush of land speculators began. Between 1979 and 1982 land values went up from $1,000–1,500 to $6,000–7,000 per dunam in the vicinity of Jewish settlements. Some Arabs could not resist the temptation, and despite local social ostracism and the death penalty imposed by Jordan on anyone selling land to Israelis, tens of thousands of dunams were sold to Israeli speculators. The sale of plots with dubious titles was carried out by straw men. Such shady operations became a national scandal when thousands of private Israelis who rushed to buy property in the West Bank from Israeli developers found themselves holding worthless scraps of paper. The Ministry of Justice stepped in and "regularized" the market by issuing an official directive for land purchase. The total area purchased by Jewish private and public bodies is estimated to have reached 100,000 dunams by 1983. Official land purchase continues. The purchase plan for 1983–1986 is to buy 31,500 dunams in seventy sites at a total expenditure of $30 million.[16]

The different methods of Israeli land seizure are of interest only to legal experts. Israeli authorities, Israeli settlers, and Palestinian inhabitants view them as one interchangeable and indistinguishable system. The land of Teqo'a settlement (east of the Etzion Block,), for example, had been designated a "military closed area" (Orders 572 and 597, of 1975); in 1980 the area became state land (1,067 dunams, declaration dated February 28, 1980). The area of Shiloh is composed of 740 dunams requisitioned for military purposes, 850 dunams declared state land, and 41 dunams expropriated for public purposes. The area of Ephrat (an urban center south of Bethlehem) comprises 710 requisitioned dunams and 1,870 dunams of declared state land.

Notes

1. Military Government, *8th Annual Report*, 1974–75, p. 120.

2. Regulations Respecting Laws and Customs of War on Land, Annex to the Convention Concerning the Laws and Customs of War on Land, Hague 1907, article 52 (emphasis added); Israeli High Court of Justice Case 606/1978.

3. For example, Prime Minister Menachem Begin in High Court of Justice Case 390/1979.

4. High Court of Justice Case 390/1979.

5. Ian Lustick, *Arabs in the Jewish State* (Austin and London: University of Texas, 1980), p. 171.

6. See *The Rule of Law in Areas Administered by Israel* (Tel Aviv: Israel National section of the International Commission of Jurists, 1981), p. 47.

7. Ibid., p. 47.

8. Quoted in Etzion regional council planning directives (August 1982), p. 22; identical statements appear in the planning directives of the Matei Binyamin regional council, sec. 4.8.

9. Pliah Albek, Director of Civil Department, State Attorney's Office Ministry of Justice, press release, September 10, 1983.

10. Lustick, *Arabs in the Jewish State*, p. 171.

11. High Court of Justice Case 285/1981.

12. Quoted in an excellent study of the land laws of Palestine and the situation in the West Bank, Raja Shehadeh, "Land Laws of Palestine," *Journal of Palestine Studies*, vol. 42 (1982), p. 79 (see also pp. 82–89), and in U. Halabi, "Expropriations in the West Bank," unpublished study supported by the West Bank Data Base Project, July 1983, p. 38. For Israeli positions, see Albek, press release, September 10, 1983.

13. William of Tyre, *A History of Deeds Done beyond the Sea*, trans. Emily Etwater Babcock and A. C. Krey, vol. 1 (New York: Columbia University Press, 1943), p. 372.

14. WZO *Plan, 1983–1986*, secs. 5.2.6, 5.2.

15. Albek, press release, September 10, 1983.

16. WZO *Plan, 1983–1986*, sec. 5.1.5.

5

The Dominant Purpose:
Legal and Administrative Considerations

Proclamation No. 2 issued by the military commander of the West Bank immediately after the occupation on June 7, 1967, stated: "*Sec. 3.* Every governmental, legislative, appointive and administrative power in respect of the region or its inhabitants shall henceforth be vested in me alone and shall only be exercised by me or by persons appointed by me for that purpose or acting on my behalf." [1]

Assuming the "authorities, duties and responsibilities vested in the local Jordanian government under the local law," explains an Israeli legal expert, "is in accordance with the requirements of international law, or specifically with article 43 of the Hague regulations and article 64 of the Fourth Geneva Convention." Israel has always maintained that the West Bank and Gaza are not "enemy territory," and therefore the Hague regulations and the Fourth Geneva Convention relating to belligerent occupation are not binding on Israel. This position is based on Israel's view that the legal status of the territories is sui generis because Jordan's sovereignty over the West Bank was never recognized internationally and Egypt never claimed sovereignty over Gaza. [2]

Israel declared, however, that it would observe de facto the humanitarian rules contained in the Hague regulations and in the Geneva Convention. Whenever the question has arisen in Israeli courts and in other forums of the status of the territories and the power of the military authorities, the Israeli authorities have stated that the relevant articles relating to belligerent occupation are being followed. The Israeli legal posture has aroused considerable political and legal controversies. International bodies, especially the International Commission of the Red Cross, took the position that the Fourth Geneva Convention applies to every occupation of territory, whatever its sovereign legal status. Political institutions, especially bodies hostile to Israel, have used the Israeli refusal to recognize the applicability of the convention as a lever for wholesale condemnation of all Israeli actions in the territories. *These legalistic controversies should not concern those who accept at face value Israel's declaration of adherence to the norms of international law and attempt to scrutinize Israel's actions in the territories in light of those norms.*

The establishment of military government is a direct result of an armed conflict. The exercise of the right of military administration has had no time limit "because it reflected a factual situation, and, pending an alternative political or military solution, this system of government could, from the legal point of view, continue forever." Its continuation expresses the needs and purposes of war, but "in addition [it expresses] the intention *not to exclude or prejudge any political solution or foreclose any rights.*" The occupant acquires exclusive control over the territory, but its posture is intrinsically temporary, pending an alternative solution. Even if the military administration continues for an indefinite period, the occupant may not treat the territories as its own, let alone acquire sovereignty over it. Indeed, the very notion of "belligerent occupant" has been introduced in international law to delegitimize the acquisition of territories (annexation) by the use of force in the course of either a defensive or an aggressive military action. Since the administration is distinctly military and constituted to pursue the occupant's belligerent aims, it may restrict, curtail, and regulate civil rights and requisition resources. These extraordinary powers must, however, be related to the basic military aim and must be reciprocated by an obligation to "do all in his power to restore and ensure, as far as possible, public order ('la vie publique') and safety, respecting at the same time, unless absolutely prevented, the laws in force in the country." [3]

Although inhabitants of the occupied territory may not claim normal civil rights, at the same time they must be assured that they are "protected," that the absolute powers are not used to perpetuate the occupation so as to prejudge any political solution—to further the political, social, and economic interests (as distinguished from the military) of the occupant and its civilian population. The norm of *status quo ante bellum* should be maintained by the occupant in exchange for absolute power. When occupation is of long duration, the freezing of the situation as it existed is impossible and impractical and may be detrimental to the occupied population, because no development or adjustment to the changing situation could take place. Even under such conditions, however, the intrinsic temporariness of the military administration must be maintained. When a change in the existing law in the West Bank was ordered by the military government, the High Court of Justice ruled:

> The provision concerning respect for the existing law requires that the Regional Commander refrain from initiating changes in the region, unless there are special reasons for doing so. Even if [these] changes do not alter the existing law, they will have a long-lasting or far-reaching effect on the situation in the Region beyond the time when the military rule in the Region comes to an end in one way or another [and therefore the action is deemed illegal].[4]

The intrinsic temporariness of the military government is expressed clearly in the Elon Moreh case: "No military government can create facts in its area for its military needs, which are designed 'ab initio' to persist even after the end of the military rule in that area, when the fate of the area, after the termination of military rule, is still not known."[5]

In light of the present discussion, it seems that we should assess Israel's actions in the West Bank and their compatibility with international law by the following tests: Has the Israeli administration taken action that implies permanent control? Has it taken actions that made permanent control more easily attainable? Would these actions not have taken place had the Israeli administration had no interest in making its control permanent? Have these actions been taken deliberately to exclude or prejudice any political solution or to foreclose any right?

I did not choose the vague expression "permanent control" at random. It is not a synonym for annexation or for the formal application of the laws of the State of Israel to the territories (Israel's procedure in Jerusalem and the Golan Heights). Permanent control means any form of administration, under whatever legal disguise, by which exclusive or ultimate control of the territories is retained and perpetuated.

During the last sixteen years many international tribunals, legal experts, political analysts, and other groups have investigated the situation in the territories and have drawn conclusions regarding actual observance of the principles of international law and the rule of law. I have not accepted as conclusive, objective, or unbiased conclusions that were based on eyewitness reports, serious studies, and well-founded legal expertise. In fact, the vast literature on legal and administrative aspects of Israeli rule in the territories has taken the form of an exchange of accusations and rebuttals and of political and legalistic polemics.

One of the reasons for the inconclusiveness of the debate (aside from the partisan perceptions of those engaged in it) has been the inconclusiveness of the evidence itself. Some actions could have been interpreted as implying permanent control, but not over the whole territory and not exclusive control. Some actions have foreclosed rights and usurped powers but could have been explained by security needs. We might assume that some actions would not have taken place unless Israel had an interest in making its control permanent, but other plausible explanations have been offered. The evidence was inconclusive because the actions themselves were based on an inconclusive conception. The Labor government, guided by the decision not to decide on the permanent disposition of the territories and by its theoretical commitment to "territorial compromise," could live with the intrinsically temporary nature of the military government. Although the actions taken strongly implied permanent control, they were not taken deliberately to exclude or to prejudice any political solutions or to foreclose any right. As long as the primary objective remained security, even in its broader definition, the Israeli High Court of Justice could accept it as a legitimate action compatible with the principles of international law.

The accession to power of the Likud government in 1977 created a new situation. Ideologically, it could not have accepted even the implied admission that the territories are "occupied." Permanent control over the land of Israel has been axiomatic for government officials. The motive and purpose of their policies has been to attain that end. The actions of the military administration have been aimed, under Likud, at making Israel's control permanent. To be sure, security and other purposes compatible with international law have been cited, and the facade of military administration has been maintained. But, as the High Court of Justice observed in the case of Elon Moreh, the dominant purpose has become political and ideological—to settle in the whole region and to "prevent the repartition of Eretz Israel." Security purposes have become secondary. "The legality of the act is judged according to the dominant purpose," stated the High Court. From now on, the actions of the military government not only imply permanent control, but "every government legislative, appointive and administrative power" has been put at the disposal of Israeli settling agencies and Jewish settlers. It seems that "ensuring public order ('la vie publique')," cited in the Hague regulations (article 43) and interpreted by legal experts as ensuring to the greatest possible extent *the good of the native population*," has been interpreted by the Israeli authorities as referring to the minuscule "Israeli settler public" and not to the Palestinian public, the original "protected population." Furthermore, actions have been taken to prejudge a political solution. I refer not to a theoretical solution but rather to an ongoing international negotiation process based on an agreed (though vague) and signed framework.[6]

The new phase began hesitantly. Although Prime Minister Menachem Begin in May 1977 promised "many more Elon Morehs," he was deeply involved in the preludes and the negotiations leading to the signing of the Camp David accords (August 1977–September 1979). The strong pressures applied by the extremist Gush Emunim group represented in the cabinet by Ariel Sharon and others were offset by the moderate foreign minister and by Defense Minister Ezer Weizman. When the Camp David accords were signed, however, and the talks on Palestinian autonomy began, the Israeli authorities initiated a systematic effort to prejudge the outcome of the negotiations. The objective had been to implement the Israeli version of the autonomy on the ground and to create the legal and administrative structure that would foreclose any other alternative. The main controversial issues in the autonomy talks (1979–1981) were the future of Jewish settlements and their status, control over natural resources and especially state land and water, the redeployment of Israeli forces, and the powers and responsibilities of the self-governing authority.

Israeli positions on these issues have been firm and unyielding. The right to settle in all parts of the land of Israel (Mandatory Palestine) was, of course, axiomatic and nonnegotiable. As for the legal status of Israeli settlements, Prime Minister Begin's autonomy proposal (March 1979) stated: "The Jewish inhabitants of Judea, Samaria and Gaza will be subject to the laws of Israel." Even Labor leaders maintained that "Jewish settlements should remain under Israeli control." Israeli leaders emphasized the importance of building settlements during the negotiations. Moshe Dayan stated in December 1978: "We should make it clear to the Americans and to others, that we intend to stay there permanently, and to make it clear, we must strengthen existing settlements and build new ones."[7]

Israel's position on state land had been that "land needed for the army and for Jewish settlements shall be under Israeli control. Uncultivated state land shall be in the hands of Israel." The redeployment of Israeli forces in "specified security locations" had been perceived by Israel as encompassing not only all the area from the West Bank watershed eastward to the River Jordan but also large areas in the central mountain massif. On an official map published in March 1981, three-quarters of the West Bank is marked "areas of security importance." The issue of the powers and responsibilities of the self-governing authority, or more specifically the source of authority, is intimately connected with Israeli status as belligerent occupant and the full rights of imperium that status entails. Israel wanted to retain such status and to grant the authority only executive powers and the power to promulgate subsidiary legislation. A ministerial committee on the autonomy decided that "the source of authority from which the Autonomy would draw its powers in the West Bank and Gaza must be Israeli."[8]

It should be noted that such Israeli positions were not formulated only for the transitional period of five years specified in the accords. *Settlements, military presence, and ultimate jurisdiction were meant to be permanent*. Although Israel stated that ''for the agreement and for peace Israel is prepared to leave the question of sovereignty open," the alternatives as the state saw them had been Israeli sovereignty or the continuation of the military government. In either case, Israel would reign supreme in the territories.[9]

It was precisely to dictate the outcome of the autonomy talks that the military government, guided by various ministerial committees and expert commissions, took a series of legal and physical actions simultaneously with the autonomy talks (1979–1981). The following actions (among others) were taken: survey of unregistered land, the approval of the new definition for state land, and the first "declarations"; massive deployment of Israeli forces and construction of infrastructure; massive settlement; transfer of responsibility over water resources from the military government to the National Water Company, Mekorot; reorganization of the function of the military government administration; cancellation of development budgets and interconnection of utility grids (water, electricity, roads); creation of Jewish regional and local councils; and creation of a civilian administration. These last two actions merit a more detailed discussion.

The Jewish Councils

On March 20, 1979, "six days before the signing of a peace treaty between Israel and Egypt," emphasizes an Israeli legal expert who was involved, the military government signed Order 783 establishing three regional councils in the West Bank. Two more regional councils were added later. An additional regional council was established in the Gaza Strip. The regulations governing the regional councils' powers and functions, defined in Order 783 as amended, are identical with the Israeli legislation.[10]

In March 1981, five local (urban) councils were established by Order 982. Their powers are identical with the powers and responsibilities of ordinary Israeli municipalities, since the order is a copy of the Israeli Municipal Ordinance (with some alterations). The regulations specify the methods of elections, voter registration, and the function of officers and employees. The council has the right to levy taxes and, aside from supplying municipal services, is empowered to carry out a wide range of activities. It is also empowered to legislate bylaws. The order establishes a municipal court of the first instance and a court of appeals. The courts operate according to Israeli procedure. Their jurisdiction is limited to bylaws and planning violations. One such court has been opened in Kiryat Arba, and the judge is a magistrate from Jerusalem. Appeals are heard by three judges from the Israeli District Court in Jerusalem. The West Bank Israeli councils were granted planning and building licensing powers (as in Israel proper). The Israeli settlement areas were declared "planning areas," and the councils were appointed as "special planning commissions." A District Planning Commission was formed, consisting of representatives of the Israeli councils and government officials.

Thus the Israeli settlements were formally separated from the "local" municipal administrative and planning system and were organized in an independent, elected, self-governing administrative and judicial system. Theoretically the powers of the Israeli councils are limited to municipal affairs. But, in Drori's words, "Because of the special status of the municipal authorities . . . and the fact that they constitute an Israeli 'island' in Judea and Samaria, there is room to consider extending the powers of these local authorities so that they may serve as channels through which the Israeli government authorities can operate." Indeed, the councils, with the active assistance of the military government and the Israeli government, have assumed quasi-governmental status. This status is clearly reflected in the jurisdictional boundaries of the councils. When Order 783 was issued, the jurisdictional (and planning) boundaries of the regional councils were defined as the combination of all the built-up areas of the settlements belonging to each council. These boundaries, which served the limited function of a regional council as a supplier of municipal services, were insufficient for the settlers and for hawkish elements in the Israeli government. "In Judea and Samaria," asserts Drori, "the determination of the boundaries of the Israeli municipal au-

thorities involves a clear political aspect; within those boundaries, only Israeli authorities will operate, and these areas will be under de facto Israeli control."[11] Accordingly, in Order 848, the definition was changed, and areas seized for military purposes and state land were added to the jurisdictional boundaries of the councils. *Later all areas liable to be declared state land were included.*

Map 7 depicts jurisdictional boundaries of the Jewish councils.

1. Local councils, whose jurisdiction is limited to the *planned* (not existing) areas of the urban centers. One council, Kiryat Arba, has a noncontiguous jurisdictional area, which corresponds to all "requisitioned" areas in the vicinity. There is a conflict of jurisdiction between that Jewish council and the Arab town of Hebron.

2. Regional councils with contiguous areas: the Jordan Valley and the Megillot (Dead Sea foreshore) councils. Most of the land has been expropriated, requisitioned, or closed or belongs to absentees. "Islands" of Arab villages and the town limits of Jericho are left out. The Hof Azza (Gaza) is also a "contiguous" council.

3. Regional councils with noncontiguous areas. The highlands of the West Bank were divided into four general areas (from north to south): Shomron, Matei Binyamin, Etzion, and Har Hebron. Within these general areas noncontiguous patches of jurisdictional areas were delineated. These irregular tracts correspond to the state land areas and are composed of all "uncultivable and unregistered lands." Most of the areas are inaccessible and are useless for settlement or for any other land use. Nevertheless, they have been painstakingly demarcated. The map makers undoubtedly felt that they were defining the areas annexed de facto to Israel. Although noncontiguous jurisdictional areas are scattered and meaningless, the overall planning responsibility of the regional councils encompasses the whole of the "general areas" allotted to them. In those areas there are Arab towns and villages with twenty times the inhabitants of the Jewish settlements. The size of this Arab population does not hinder the regional councils from defining planning principles and from implementing them with the assistance of the military government. In fact, the "general areas" of the regional councils are for all intents and purposes a Jewish administrative division of the West Bank, unrelated and separate from the Arab subdistrict administrative division. Map 9 shows the "dual" ethnic administrative division of the West Bank.

The Israeli ministries use the councils to provide state services: the budgetary allocations for such services are incorporated in the general budgets of the Israeli civilian ministries. Standards are identical with those applied in Israel. In education, welfare, and religious services, the standards applied to the Jewish councils are more generous than in Israel, especially as far as employment of teachers and officials is concerned. In some settlements, more than one-third of the householders receive their salary from government sources.

In addition, the councils are involved in all high-level decisions on infrastructure and on legal, economic, security, and land and water matters in the West Bank. Regional councils establish "development corporations" and form a strong lobby through the Council of Jewish Settlements in Judea and Samaria. They form an imperium in imperio because of their de facto powers and the fact they are exposed neither to the control, checks, and balances and scrutiny of the Israeli political system nor to the authority of the military government.

To be sure, the military authorities dutifully publish orders, amendments, and regulations concerning a variety of civilian matters relating to the councils and the Jewish settlements therein. The group of people who head the councils, however, has a better direct and multilevel access to the Israeli centers of power than does the military government. This group does not rely on the military for budgets, and its representatives actually participate in the meetings of the Ministerial Committee on Settlements. After all, they represent the "dominant purpose." No wonder the military government has abdicated its powers and authority not only on matters concerning the life of the settlements but also on all matters pertaining to the territories except military, political, administrative, and development control of the Arab population.

Even in strictly security matters, the Jewish settlers form a quasi-independent force. When "security" is defined in the broadest terms—and there is an established tradition of identifying presence in civilian settlements with active military duty—the borderline between a citizen and a soldier becomes increasingly ambiguous. All the settlements on the West Bank and Gaza are defined as "border settlements" in which, according to Military Order 432 and other orders, guards are authorized to exercise force and, among other things, to open fire, though only at certain times and places, that is, when they are on guard duty and in reaction to a well-defined cause. Many residents of the West Bank are, in fact, conscripts "on extended leave," mainly religious students combining military service with rabbinical studies. In every settlement a settler is appointed "security. officer" and receives a salary from the Ministry of Defense or from the Israeli police. The councils have formed security committees that "coordinate security matters."

The settlements (or, as they are called in army jargon, "confrontation settlements") are organized within the framework of the Territorial Defense Unit of the IDF. That framework is not limited to the self-defense of isolated and distant settlements. As the network of settlements became increasingly dense, the emphasis was transferred from the perimeter of the individual settlement to cultivated fields, access roads, and the guarding of economic and community facilities. The settlements are clustered into "forward sectors" with a combined command in the rear.

The units of the settlements' territorial defense are supposed to delay the potential enemy until the arrival of army units (either regular forces or reserve forces) from farther away. Every settlement has an allotted number of fit combatants, among them officers. All males are reserve soldiers whose active duty is done in the settlements on a part-time basis while the soldiers lead a normal civilian life. They were transferred to the territorial defense from their original units in the infantry, the armored corps, the artillery, or the combat engineering corps. The members of the territorial defense units in the "confrontation settlements" are considered high-quality reserve forces who know the combat area well and are highly motivated to defend their own homes. Some of the officers and men objected to being transferred from their old combat units to the territorial defense units. When they appealed to the chief of staff, Raphael Eitan, who initiated the reorganization, he ended the argument by issuing a direct order.

The units of the territorial defense are organized in regional "hedgehogs," which defend strategic areas and possible avenues of attack. An officer and a small number of soldiers are stationed within the borders of the settlement for contiguous defense and to allow for the maintenance of economic activities. Every unit of the regional defense has a mobile force equipped with armored personnel carriers. The mobile force is composed of combatants assembled from three settlements so as not to bring together the residents of a single settlement in a framework in which serious casualties could destroy an entire settlement. These combined mobile units are employed in "current security" activities, which in military jargon means policing the Palestinian population. The Judea Company, consisting of settlers in the Hebron Mountains, is notorious for its brutal treatment of the Arab populations.

Reserve soldiers within the territorial defense are prepared for mobilization on very short notice, including by telephone, and can reach their posts, their weapons, and their ammunition quickly. They keep their personal arms with them (like all reserve officers and many soldiers, if they so wish); heavier arms are stored in the settlement armories. Settlements in the rear that are located in the midst of "hostile populations" are also organized in the territorial defense, but urban settlements whose residents work (and frequently sleep) outside the borders of the settlement find it more difficult to allocate the necessary military manpower and to call up reserve soldiers in the case of a sudden alert. In urban settlements the weapons are meant to defend the lives of those who are equipped with them and are not for "out-of-the-fence" duties.

The standing orders and written procedures do not present an obstacle to personal interpretation on the part of those who bear arms or those who exercise authority and instruct the security forces to deviate from those instructions. In February 1983 a military court severely criticized the illegal orders of senior officers on the West Bank and apparently also those of the chief of staff, Raphael Eitan. As in other aspects of Israeli security on the West Bank, the dry letter of the law leaves considerable room for maneuver, sometimes enough to reverse declared policies completely.

The quasi-independence of ideologically motivated armed settlers, serving part time under their own commanders, has led to various vigilante activities, including the smashing of cars and harassment of the Arab population. The degree of independence of the armed settlers and the lack of control over their activities were revealed by an Israeli official committee. The committee found that incidents of vigilantism (vandalizing of Arab property, opening fire, and harassment) had not been investigated "because of intervention of politicians, including senior members of the government coalition, who have caused investigation to be called off by intervening with authorities." A former chief of internal security who was responsible for investigating vigilante activity (including the attempt on West Bank mayors' lives), went even further. He stated, "There is heavy suspicion that Jewish terrorist groups find shelter in Jewish settlements in the West Bank, where there is a sympathetic political environment. . . . Those settlers who took the law into their hands and established illegal settlements have now become legitimate. . . . This proved to them that 'destroyers of fences' and lawbreakers have been right, that they have become strong and respectable."[12]

The present legal status of the settlements is ambiguous. Nowhere is it determined that the settlements are *not* under the jurisdiction of the existing Jordanian law. This omission, however, is considered an anomaly that is constantly being ironed out. The process of rectifying "judicial anomalies" aimed at abolishing the difference (termed "discrimination") between the status of settlers in the West Bank and ordinary Israeli citizens is slow and deals with particular issues rather than with general principles. It is,

however, consistent and extended. The method used is the emendation of the Israeli law, the application of specific laws and regulations to the Israeli residents of the West Bank, the publication of military orders that apply only to residents of Israeli settlements, or extralegal arrangements.

In 1980 the Knesset passed an amendment (No. 8) to the Israeli income tax ordinance by which the income of an Israeli citizen that is produced in the territories or received there is considered as if its source had been in Israel and as if it had been received in Israel. The regulation suggests that the territories cannot be a tax shelter for Israeli citizens. In reality, they became a paradise of legal tax evasion. It appears that a taxpayer who lives in the territories and continues to refuse to pay income tax cannot be forced to pay, since Israel has no authority to apply enforcement measures in a foreign country (in this case, the West Bank). In theory the income tax authorities could of course wait for the recalcitrant taxpayer at the Green Line, and, as soon as he crossed it, he could be arrested and his debt collected. The State of Israel actually took the initiative, however, in alleviating the tax burden of Israelis who live in the territories. In most of the settlements, even those that are very near the Green Line, the settlers are granted a reduction of 7 percent in income tax up to a certain income. Purchase tax also does not apply in the territories, nor does land registry tax, which amounts to more than 3 percent of the total cost of an apartment. Capital gain on the sale of property does not apply to the West Bank, and Israeli residents there are allowed to hold foreign currency freely (in Jordanian dinars, which are legal tender in the West Bank). It is incomparably cheaper to hire people in the West Bank than in Israel. Employers' tax, which comes to 7 percent, does not apply there; nor is it compulsory to insure Arab workers employed in Jewish enterprises with the National Insurance Institute (at a cost of as much as 15 percent of the salaries). An Israeli company is required to pay income tax even if it functions on the West Bank or is registered there if control of the company is in Israel. Israeli companies, however, register holding companies in Ramallah and Nablus under Jordanian law. These daughter companies in turn control other new companies that are also registered in the West Bank. Expert opinion holds that the "granddaughter" companies have to pay tax only according to Jordanian law, which imposes a lower tax than that paid by ordinary Israeli companies. When and if these loopholes are closed, a new problem will arise. Israelis will complain that they are "discriminated against in comparison to the Arabs," who continue to pay lower Jordanian taxes.

Israelis might complain about discrimination in taxation. At present, however, they benefit from all rights of the Israeli welfare state system, receiving benefits denied to the Palestinian population. According to the regulations of the National Insurance Institute, a qualified "insured person" must reside in Israel. Israeli residents in the territories, however, are entitled by an extralegal arrangement to the full range of National Insurance Institute benefits. West Bankers employed in Israel, by contrast, are eligible for insurance covering only accidents at work. Israeli residents in the territories collect unemployment allowances, although residence in Israel is required by law. The law for encouragement of capital investment applies only to the boundaries of Israel, and the official development zoning of the country determines the degree of government aid. By an extralegal arrangement, investment in the territories receives the highest level of "encouragement" under the law. When Jewish wives in the territories complained that Israeli domestic appliance service companies refused to service their products because the owners resided "outside Israel," the minister of trade and industry issued an emergency regulation that extended the insurance obligation for appliances to the Jewish settlements in the territories. The growth of the Jewish suburban centers will require faster and more radical legal action and will perhaps force the government to enact general legislation that will apply Israeli laws and administration to the areas of the regional councils or to the citizens residing therein.

On January 2, 1984, the Israeli Knesset passed a law amending and extending Emergency Regulations, Judea and Samaria, Gaza and South Sinai (1967). Article 4 of the regulations now reads (unofficial translation):

> 4. After regulation 6a insert:
> 6b(a) For the purpose of the enactments set out in the schedule, the term "resident of Israel" or any other term denoting residence, domicile or living in Israel mentioned therein, will be viewed as including both a person whose place of residence is in the Area and is an Israeli citizen, or is entitled to immigrate to Israel under the Law of Return 1950, and who, if his place of residence were in Israel, would come under the said definition.
> (b) The Minister of Justice with the confirmation of the Constitution and Law Committee of the Knesset, may change the schedule by order.[13]

The "Area" denotes Judea and Samaria (the West Bank) and Gaza; "entitled to immigrate to Israel under the Law of Return 1950" denotes persons of the Jewish religion. Being a beneficiary of the ten laws mentioned in the "schedule" is conditional upon residence in Israel, or upon being a citizen of Israel. With the passing of this law, the personal status of Jewish settlers in the territories has been "equalized" to the

status of Israeli citizens and Jews residing in Israel proper. Article (b) points to future developments. The minister of justice was empowered to "change the schedule by order," which means that additions to the existing Israeli laws that already apply to the territories has become a routine matter, needing only secondary legislation. It is not inconceivable that the minister would dispense with the "schedule," replacing it with the phrase, "for the purpose of *any law*." When and if such an amendment is promulgated in the Israeli Knesset, the trend toward a dual legislative, judicial, and administrative system in the territories would be formally completed. Even without such a drastic measure, however, the dual system, part for the Jews and part for the Arabs, has already become a well-established and institutionalized fact.

The Civilian Administration

The legal act that institutionalized the permanent Israeli system of control over the Palestinians in the territories is Military Order 947 (November 8, 1981), establishing a civilian administration. This order has correctly been termed by Shehadeh and Kuttab "a unilateral declaration of constitutive change."[14]

The task of the civilian administration is to "see to the civilian affairs of the *local* residents; this while paying heed to consideration of public order."[15] By Order 947 the administrative system of the military government was changed, separating military and security matters from civilian affairs. A head of the civilian administration was appointed by the commander of the Israel Defense Forces in the area. His powers include all the powers set forth in the "local" (Jordanian) law, except for military powers set forth in such laws and all the civilian powers set forth in the "security legislation" (military government orders). The area commander retains the prerogative to enact primary legislation, and the head of the civilian administration is granted the power of enacting subsidiary legislation, appointing staff officers and government employees, and delegating authority to them.

Order 947 did not at first blush appear to change the administrative setup in the West Bank, since the separation between the civilian administration (staff officers) and the military headquarters existed long before its publication. The radical change brought about by the order, however, should be appreciated in the political context of the Camp David agreement and the positions of Israel in the autonomy talks.[16]

The Camp David agreement calls for the "withdrawal" of the "Israeli military government and its civilian administration as soon as a self-governing authority has been freely elected." The Egyptian (and American) position has been that the military government must be abolished and replaced by the self-governing authority. In Order 947 the Israelis, by a stroke of the pen, tried to impose their own interpretation. They did so by simply replacing the title military commander of the West Bank (Judea and Samaria) with commander of the Israeli Forces in Judea and Samaria. The West Bank ceased to be a separate military government district and became an area in which Israeli forces under the officer commanding the Central Command are stationed, just as they are stationed in the area of Tel Aviv. Not only was the separate military government abolished, but it was also withdrawn because the headquarters of the Central Command are situated outside the West Bank. This withdrawal, however, does not mean that the military government jurisdiction is abolished. One of the most controversial issues in the autonomy negotiations is that of the source of authority: Who retains the legislative power in the West Bank, and what specifically is the meaning of "transfer of authority" from the military government to the self-governing authority? Order 947 is meant to impose the Israeli position; that is, the Israeli military government, represented by the commander of the IDF in the area, will retain all the powers he assumed in Proclamation 2 of June 1967. The head of the civilian administration is left with powers only to legislate subsidiary legislation and is always subordinate to the higher authority of the military government. This state of affairs matches precisely the powers that Israel plans to grant the self-governing authority.

The issue of the legal validity of military government orders in the so-called transition period was also discussed in the autonomy talks, and the Egyptian position was that with the transfer of authority, all such orders would automatically be abolished. To forestall this eventuality, Order 947 raised all "security legislation" (military government orders) to the status of substantive law (paragraph 3b), thereby making them equal in status to the Jordanian law and an integral part of the permanent law of the land. The powers delegated to the head of the civilian administration are all the powers set forth in the Jordanian law (except for security-related matters) and 162 military orders of a civilian nature. Orders 783 and 892 (concerning Jewish councils) are included, but the powers of the civilian administration head concerning the Jewish regional and local councils are nominal and theoretical, since these bodies are directly linked to the Israeli ministries. The separation is clear also from the fact that the budget of the civilian administration is part of the budget of the Ministry of Defense, whereas the councils' budgets are included in the budgets of the civilian ministries.

The authority granted the head of the civilian administration to delegate powers and to appoint officials is also significant. It should be examined against the background of the wholesale transfer of executive powers from local officials to Israeli staff officers. This policy of transfer of powers began soon after the occupation. Numerous orders transferred the powers of the Jordanian king and the Jordanian ministries, as well as those of local officers, boards, and local semigovernmental bodies, to Israeli officials. Moreover, important matters were removed from the jurisdiction of local courts and were vested in Israeli military courts and tribunals. By 1981 the concentration of almost all executive powers was complete, and the head of the civilian administration was in a position to delegate extensive executive powers to local inhabitants who were prepared to cooperate.

The attempt to predetermine the outcome of the autonomy talks is clear enough. The import of the establishment of the civilian administration, however, extends beyond its immediate political and administrative significance. Concealed in the legal phrases of Order 947 lies a fundamental turning point in Israel's system of control over the Palestinians in the territories. The civilian administration constitutes *the transformation from a temporary to a permanent system*. There is nothing new in the system itself: it is the old and well-practiced system of control of the Israeli Arabs extended to embrace 1.3 million additional Palestinians. An analysis of this fundamental aspect of the civil administration requires a historical description.

The 1948 war destroyed Palestinian society and left the most backward elements of that society in Israel, without its elites and lacking any social or economic cohesion. The policies adopted by the Israeli government toward the Arab minority were geared to maintain ecological, cultural, and social separation, to fight cohesive processes by forced segmentation of the population (Druze, Christian villages, townsfolk), institutionalizing economic dependence and the co-optation of "positive elements." Israeli Arab society never gained independence and remained a subordinate group, outside the pale of Israeli society.[17] In the area occupied by Jordan, the Hashemites employed the same policies of segmentation, economic dependence, and co-optation to attain total incorporation into the Jordanian system by destroying independent Palestinian society and stifling Palestinian national aspirations. The Jordanian efforts were not entirely successful, however, and after the occupation the Israelis found a cohesive Palestinian society in the West Bank with weakened but still powerful elites wielding political and administrative power and possessing considerable economic viability.

Moshe Dayan, the defense minister who shaped Israel's policies in the territories and remained the territories' supreme ruler for the first formative years, with his keen intuitive perceptions sensed the difference between the segmented, leaderless Israeli Arab community and the Palestinian society in the West Bank. He loathed the policies of the Arabist administrators and military governors who controlled the Israeli Arab community, and he therefore refused categorically to allow them to extend their jurisdiction to the occupied territories. Instead he appointed regular and reserve combat officers and entrusted them with the dual role of military commanders and civilian administrators. His instructions were clear and concise: "Let the Arabs rule themselves as far as possible. Don't try to interpose an Israeli administration." [18] He accepted as given the existence of a Palestinian society and began a dialogue with its traditional elite.

The administration was molded to serve Dayan's noninterventionist policy. The local (district) military governor, who dealt directly with the population, was subordinate to two parallel authority structures and wore two hats: the military and the civilian. His job was to maintain order and security by using the soldiers at his disposal. On the other hand, he was also responsible for civilian activity, including liaison with the Palestinian authorities, mainly the municipalities, the village councils, and the chambers of commerce. The local commander was subordinate to two parallel superiors: to his own brigade commander and through him to the chief of staff. He was simultaneously subordinate to the military governor of the West Bank (or Gaza), whose prime responsibility was civilian affairs. The military governor was subordinate to the coordinator of activities in the territories, a general staff officer directly under the minister of defense. The two chains of command converged only in the defense minister's office, giving Dayan the power to dictate policies and to see them carried through.

This period (1967–1974) was characterized by absolute centralization. The civil arm and the military arm were not permitted to decide on military or civilian matters separately. In general during the period, civilian considerations took precedence except on issues touching strictly upon security. The difference between the two arms had no practical significance because at the top level (the minister of defense) and at the bottom level (the district governor) they were fused together.

The policy of nonintervention was based on dialogue with the existing traditional power centers, represented by the mayors of Palestinian towns. These mayors were appointed by the Jordanian regime and were loyal to it and traditionally pragmatic and moderate. The 1967–1974 period was characterized by an informal dual Israeli-Jordanian rule in the West Bank, where the Palestinian mayors served as liaison between Israel and Jordan and benefited from financial assistance from both countries. It was in the interests of both countries to maintain the existing leadership and to prevent the emergence of a radical PLO-ori-

ented alternative leadership. This policy was also compatible with Dayan's pragmatic approach, which in essence sought to safeguard Israeli interests while leaving Jordanians to deal with the population. The functional rather than territorial partition, combined with liberal policies (lack of political censorship, opening of universities, permission to engage in limited political activities, development of an agricultural support system), gained the military government a reputation for benign occupation. The fact that during Dayan's reign hundreds of Palestinians were expelled, houses were demolished, and land was seized was generally ignored because the military administration at the time conformed to the main principle of belligerent occupation by being temporary and by maintaining the *status quo ante bellum*. To be sure, Dayan's intention was to perpetuate the arrangement and to turn it into a long-term political pragmatic solution. The relative calm, the economic prosperity, the expulsion of the PLO from Jordan in September 1970, and the continued dialogue with the Hashemites gave hope that, indeed, the temporary arrangement would last. Nationalistic sentiment, however, was simmering beneath the surface. It erupted in April 1973 after the Israelis raided Beirut and killed PLO leaders. The depth of anti-Israel sentiments expressed in demonstrations, violence, and public prayers shocked the military government, which had assumed that the population had become reconciled to the benign occupation. Soon afterward the last Israeli illusions were shattered by the October 1973 war. The radicalization of the Palestinian population grew with the political ascendancy of the PLO and seriously threatened the traditional, pragmatic, and moderate elites. The resolution of the Rabat Conference (1974) that the PLO is the sole representative of the Palestinian people forced Jordan into a defensive position. The Israeli position vis-à-vis the territories hardened, and Dayan, the architect of the military government, resigned.

Dayan's successor, Shimon Peres, who lacked Dayan's intuitive genius, tried to pursue the same policies. When he allowed municipal elections to be held in 1976, however, the old elites were squarely defeated. The PLO decided to participate in the elections, and six radical mayors were elected. The radicalization of the situation was expressed in increased violence, and the military government entered its second phase (1976–1981).

The administrative reaction to the new situation was the transfer of the military arm to the direct command of the governor of the West Bank, who had previously dealt with civilian affairs. The full integration of military and civilian tasks was perceived as an efficient means of fighting radical elements, in both the security and the political arenas. The administrative aspects became secondary, and Israeli and Palestinian administrators embarked on a collision course.

The radical mayors started their terms by trying to retain the image of public servants and proving that they were more efficient than their "corrupt and docile" predecessors. The increased political tension caused by the accession of the Likud government and the Jewish settlements, however, forced them to abandon the technocratic posture and to assume a distinctly political role.

The Israeli administration helped push the mayors into their political position. When radical mayors requested budget allocations and licenses, the military governors began to use delaying tactics or refused their request, hoping that the population would blame the mayors for the hardships that ensued. Furthermore, the Israelis began using tactics of harassment against the Palestinian leaders, such as house arrests, summonses, and interrogations aimed at humiliation. Such treatment enhanced the political prestige of the mayors, however. The categorical refusal of the Palestinian leadership to participate in any way in the peace process, the wholesale land seizure, violent incidents, and the increased tension between the "rejectionists" and pro-Jordanian and more moderate PLO supporters in 1978–1980 brought the unrest and confrontation to its peak. When Defense Minister Ezer Weizman resigned and Prime Minister Begin assumed his position, Chief of Staff Raphael Eitan seized the opportunity to put the coordinator of activities under his command, thus achieving the final demise of the civilian arm. The professional civilian staff officers were left to their own devices with no political direction except "control" and with budgets that had been curtailed and in many cases had been canceled altogether. Raphael Eitan initiated a policy termed "the iron fist," which some soldiers, officers, and vigilantes understood as a license to commit brutal acts. Other officers, however, objected to the policies of intimidation and observed that it is impossible to solve a political problem by military means.

We should examine the creation of the civilian administration against this background. The civilian administration was meant to provide the missing political element that, combined with military measures, would combat the influence of the PLO and would coerce the Palestinians into accepting the permanent status of a subordinate minority.

Within the framework of Likud policies, there has been no role for Jordan in the West Bank, either as the "cofunctional ruler" that Dayan envisaged or (of course) as a partner for a territorial compromise. An independent Palestinian state is anathema. "Full territorial autonomy" is rejected as tending to form the nucleus of a PLO state. The only tolerated political solution therefore became Begin's "autonomy for the

inhabitants." The Palestinians, however, rejected this formula categorically. Enter an Arabist, who not only provided the theoretical background and the strategy but was ready to implement it. The Palestinians, argued Menachem Milson, are intimidated by the PLO, which, through terror, bribery, and ostracism, seized political control in the territories. Moderate Arabs willing to come forth and to begin a serious dialogue based on Israel's autonomy plan are afraid, and the blame rests on the shoulders of Moshe Dayan and his successors, who accepted his policy of nonintervention. That policy permitted PLO mayors to use the administrative and political power of their office to stifle all attempts at moderation. The policy of nonintervention was disastrous, Milson maintained, because it is based on total ignorance of the Arab civic mentality. Arab social interaction is based on patronage (*wasta*), and without active intervention through a system of patronage, Arabs cannot be ruled. The Turks, the British, and the Jordanians operated on that basis, and Dayan's policies ruined the system. Since the old traditional elites were ousted by the PLO-oriented educated townsfolk, an alternative elite should be created from the peasants, who constitute 70 percent of the population. Village notables could be cultivated by delegating powers and dispensing patronage. Simultaneously, mayors who refused to cooperate should be removed from their administrative power bases and their followers punished. "Combatting the PLO in the territories had been perceived by the Israeli policy-makers as a military and security matter," wrote Milson, "while the PLO attach a special *political* importance to its quest for influence in the territories. . . . [Its success] facilitated the mobilization of people for terrorist acts." Therefore, "a political infrastructure opposed to the PLO and ready to cooperate with Israel" should be created, and military pressure should be increased simultaneously. This had been the objective of the civilian government, and Milson was called upon to implement his theories as the first head of the civilian administration.[19]

The creation of the civilian administration completely separated the military arm from the civilian arm, and civilians were appointed both as coordinator of activities and as head of the administration. Two separate bureaucracies had begun to execute different and contradictory orders, and personal rivalries created administrative confusion. Supporters of the new system claimed, however, that the separation of civilian and military functions enabled each arm to take care of its own tasks and eliminated a situation whereby the military arm took precedence. All these excuses were given after the fact, since the creation of the head of the civilian administration was a political decision. At any rate, the Palestinian subjects have discerned no difference because, from their point of view, both bureaucracies act in unison. Indeed, the iron fist policies of the military had been complemented by a series of coercive civilian measures. The mayors who understood Milson's objectives refused to cooperate and boycotted the head of the civilian administration. The administration responded by dismissing first three and later six mayors, whereupon the rest suspended all municipal activities in protest. The administration, whose effort to coerce the mayors had failed, hailed the result as a success. The dismissal of the mayors and the appointment of Israeli officers as administrators of Palestinian towns were presented as part of a plan to remove the PLO from positions of administrative and political power. The confrontation with the mayors was followed by blocking the flow of Jordanian-PLO funds, which halted all development projects, since the civilian administration directed its meager budget to the rural areas. Long blacklists of people were prepared to deny them even simple services, such as driving licenses. The attempt to fragment the political elite was complemented by an attempt to create an alternative elite in the form of the village leagues.

The civil government had found a Hebron village league in existence (established August 1978) and embarked upon its expansion of all parts of the West Bank. Within four years a Movement of Palestinian Leagues had been organized in seven regional districts. The expansion was achieved by investing the rural leaders with powers of patronage, development budgets, and arms to form private militias. Villagers and townsfolk were sent by civilian administration officials to officers of the leagues to secure recommendations without which building licenses and permits for travel and family reunions could not be obtained. Village league recommendations helped to curtail prison terms and to remove people from blacklists. Development budgets denied to towns were freely given to villages that supported the leagues. Village league spokesmen obliged by issuing anti-PLO and pro–Camp David statements. Israeli government spokesmen introduced the village leagues as the "nascent administration" of the self-governing authority. When the autonomy issue became irrelevant and President Reagan announced his new peace initiative in October 1982, the civilian administration gave the village leagues a new role: to prevent pro-Hashemite Palestinians from expressing agreement with King Hussein's anticipated willingness to join the peace process.

The civilian administration has found surrogates to carry out its policy of control. Its prime objective, the creation of an alternative elite, however, has not been attained. The village leagues could not broaden their narrow social base and were led by people who were viewed as disreputable. It seems that the failure

was caused by two erroneous assumptions: first, that Palestinian unwillingness to accept the assigned role of a subordinate minority resulted from PLO intimidation and terror, and, second, that Jordan would oblige and support the leagues because the leagues combat the PLO. The Jordanian decision of March 1982 to make membership in the leagues an act of treason dealt a severe blow to the chances of recruiting pro-Jordanian villagers. The townsfolk, being PLO supporters, view the leagues as quislings and treat them with contempt.

Milson's successors seem to be disillusioned with the prospect of attaining the objective of an alternative elite. Still, they continue to use the leagues as an instrument of control. At the same time the civilian administration continues its policies of segmentation and the undermining of the social and economic base of Palestinian nationalism.

It is ironic that although the system of control applied to Israeli Arabs is weakening and is costly to maintain, the same system is being vigorously applied in the territories. In the absence of any political solution except permanent control of the territories, the Israelis view this option as the only one.

Notes

1. West Bank Military Government, Collection of Proclamations and Orders, Proclamation no. 2, sec. 3, June 7, 1967.

2. *The Rule of Law in Areas Administered by Israel* (Tel Aviv: Israel National Section of the International Commission of Jurists, 1981), p. 1.

3. The first two quoted statements appear in Meir Shamgar, *Military Government in the Territories* (Jerusalem: Hebrew University, 1982), pp. 44–45 (emphasis added here and in subsequent quotations). The occupant's duties are set forth as quoted in Hague regulations, article 43.

4. High Court of Justice case 351/80.

5. Elon Moreh case; High Court of Justice case 390/79.

6. High Court of Justice case 390/79; Proclamation no. 2; G. von Glahn, *The Occupation of Enemy Territory: A Commentary on the Law and Practice of Belligerent Occupation* (Minneapolis: University of Minnesota, 1957), pp. 33–34.

7. Menachem Begin, *Haaretz*, March 8, 1979; Moshe Dayan, quoted by Arieh Shalev, "The Autonomy—Problems and Possible Solutions, Center for Strategic Studies, Tel Aviv University, no. 8, 1979 (mimeographed), p. 115.

8. *Haaretz*, April 19, 1979.

9. Quoted by Shalev, "Autonomy," pp. 62–64.

10. Moshe Drori, "The Israeli Settlements in Judea and Samaria: Legal Aspects," in Daniel J. Elazar, ed., *Judea, Samaria, and Gaza: Views on the Present and Future* (Washington, D.C.: American Enterprise Institute, 1982), p. 60.

11. Drori, "Israeli Settlements," pp. 66, 64.

12. Karp Committee, *Jerusalem Post*, May 17, 1983; David Achituv, *Davar*, August 19, 1983. The full Karp report was published February 7, 1984.

13. State of Israel Bill 1656, December 14, 1983 (text); *Haaretz*, January 3, 1983 (Knesset debate).

14. Jonathan Kuttab and Raja Shehadeh, *Civilian Administration in the Occupied West Bank*, Ramallah, West Bank, 1982, p. 18.

15. Ibid., p. 23.

16. See *Jerusalem Post*, January 20, 1980.

17. See Ian Lustick, *Arabs in the Jewish State* (Austin and London: University of Texas, 1980).

18. Shabtai Teveth, *The Cursed Blessing* (Jerusalem and Tel Aviv: Schocken, 1970), p. 28.

19. Menachem Milson, *Is There a Solution to the Palestinian Problem?* (Jerusalem: Van Leer Institute, 1982), pp. 42, 43.

6

From Security to Suburbia: Israeli Settlements in the West Bank

By September 1983, 106 Israeli settlements had been established in the West Bank and Gaza (excluding East Jerusalem). As map 10 shows, 98 are situated in the West Bank; 8 are in the Gaza Strip. Of the West Bank settlements 15 are Nahal (paramilitary) outposts. The number of housing (family) units in the settlements (occupied, vacant, and under construction) was, in the summer of 1983, 12,731; there were 12,427 in the West Bank and 304 in Gaza. The number of families was estimated in September 1983 at 6,500 (27,500 persons) settled in the West Bank and 200 (900 persons) in the Gaza Strip. The settlements are scattered throughout the West Bank; in the Gaza Strip they are clustered in the southwestern coastal area.

Israeli settlements are officially grouped in two broad categories (excluding paramilitary outposts, which would constitute a third category): urban-suburban and rural-semiurban. Urban settlements include the following types:

1. The city is a strong urban community serving as regional, industrial, service, and cultural center. Its population consists of more than 10,000 families (42,000 persons), and it encompasses an area of 7,000–15,000 dunams.
2. The *kiriya* (town) is an urban center of 3,000–5,000 families (12,000–20,000 persons) and a subregional service center, with low-density housing. Its planned area is 2,500–5,000 dunams.
3. The *toshava* (suburb) is a satellite neighborhood serving as a commuter dormitory, with minimal local services but with good access to major metropolitan areas. It lies within thirty minutes' driving distance of existing urban centers. Its planned area is 500–2,000 dunams (500–2,000 families, or 2,500–8,500 persons).

Urban settlements are planned by the Ministry of Housing or by private developers. Housing units are individually purchased (see "Public Financing" for

discussion of incentives). *Toshavot* are planned and built by private developers with varying degrees of government assistance.

Rural-semiurban settlements also include several types.

1. The *yishuv kehilati* is a nonagricultural cooperative settlement established by the World Zionist Organization, which provides infrastructure, housing, and basic industry. The settlement is "handed over" to a settler group (*gar'in*) that forms a cooperative with its own internal regulations. New members must be approved by existing members and must go through a one-year internship period. Employment is mainly outside the settlement (and entails commuting), although 15 percent of households are expected to work in production branches on the site. "Clusters" of *yishuvim kehilatiim* are planned to form a *kiriya*. The planned population size is 200–300 families (800–1,200 persons) on an area of 400–800 dunams. This cooperative settlement is affiliated with the Gush Emunim settlement movement (Amana).

2. The agricultural cooperatives are traditional forms of rural settlements (kibbutz, *moshav, moshav shitufi*), all based on agriculture and industry, with on-site production and collective ownership (to varying degrees) of the means of production. The planned size of settlement is 80–160 families (350–650 persons), for a built-up area similar in size to the *kehilati*. The cultivated area ranges between 3,000 and 5,000 dunams. The agricultural cooperative is affiliated with various national settlement movements; it was established by and is supported by the World Zionist Organization.

3. The settlement center (*mercaz ikhlus*) is an undefined housing estate planned to form the nucleus of a settlement. When sufficient settlers are gath-

TABLE 12

HOUSING UNITS AND FAMILIES IN THE WEST BANK, BY
SETTLEMENT TYPE, 1982

Type of Settlement	Units	Families	Ratio of Occupancy (units per family)
Urban	8,808	2,911	3.0
Rural-semiurban	3,478	2,144	1.6
Nahal outpost	141	75	1.9
Total	12,427	5,130	2.4

SOURCE: World Zionist Organization, *Development Plan, 1983–1986.*

ered, they decide on the type of permanent settlement.

In September 1982 there were eighteen urban settlements of all types with nearly 3,000 families and sixty-five rural-semiurban settlements of all types with about 2,100 families. The distribution of housing units (existing and under construction) by settlement type appears in table 12.

The difference in ratio of occupancy between urban and rural settlements stems from the fact that the housing figures in the urban areas reflect a very high proportion of building starts and even units in pre-construction stages (infrastructure preparation). In rural settlements, however, the ratio of 1.6 units per family reflects a high proportion of completed but vacant units.

The classification of Israeli settlements by settlement type is at this stage of development of rather limited significance. Many planned towns have smaller populations than some of the larger *yishuvim kehilatiim*, and some rural settlements are in the process of turning into suburban estates. The classification serves mainly bureaucratic purposes, since each type is under the jurisdiction of a different Israeli agency. Cities and towns are handled by the Ministry

of Housing, *toshavot* are under the Ministry of Agriculture, and rural settlements are under the auspices of the World Zionist Organization. Each of these types receives different incentives, and until recently their planning had not been coordinated. Of much more significance is the classification of Israeli settlements by geographic region.

The West Bank is divided in official Israeli documents into three zones, on the basis of "demand"—that is, decreasing intensity of "diffused processes" emanating from natural demand created in the central region (Tel Aviv conurbation) and in Jerusalem—for better housing and industrial development. The high-demand zone is defined in terms of travel time to metropolitan centers on an optimal road network: thirty minutes' travel time from the settlements to the inner ring of cities in the Tel Aviv conurbation and twenty minutes' travel time to Jerusalem. The medium-demand zone stretches from the outer perimeter of the high-demand zone in the west to fifty minutes' travel time from Tel Aviv and thirty-five minutes from Jerusalem. The low-demand zone stretches east and south of the medium-demand zone up to the Jordan River and the Dead Sea foreshore.

This socioeconomic definition corresponds to a geographic division of the West Bank into the foothills, the mountain massif, and the Jordan Rift Valley. (There are two exceptions: the Jerusalem area is part of the western high-demand region, and south Judea is part of the eastern low-demand zone.) Henceforth, I shall refer to the following geographical divisions: the metropolitan, the central massif, and the rift regions (see maps 5 and 11).

As table 13 makes clear, two-thirds of the housing units are situated in the metropolitan areas. The reason is evident: the eastern region is occupied by small rural settlements, whereas the metropolitan area is urban. The importance of the information contained in table 13, however, goes beyond these details. The 1982 data illustrate the achievement in the initial phases of Israeli settlement activity and also indicate a

TABLE 13

DISTRIBUTION OF SETTLEMENTS, HOUSING UNITS, AND FAMILIES IN THE WEST BANK, BY REGION, 1982

	Rift and South Judea			Central Massif			Metropolitan			Total		
	Settlements	Housing units	Families	Settlements	Housing units	Families	Settlements	Housing units	Families	Settlements	Housing units	Families
Total	40	1,637	987	21	2,165	1,346	37	8,625	2,797	98	12,427	5,130
Urban	1	264	240	3	1,294	906	14	7,250	1,765	18	8,808	2,911
Rural-semiurban	26	1,232	672	16	871	440	23	1,375	1,032	65	3,478	2,144
Paramilitary	13	141	75	2	—	—	—	—	—	15	141	75

SOURCE: WZO *Plan 1983–1986.*

turning point and the start of a new, and perhaps the most crucial, settlement phase. I shall describe and analyze each of the three phases of Israeli settlement activity—the Allon, the Gush Emunim, and the suburban phase—in turn.

The Initial Phase: The Allon Settlement Plan

The initial phase of Israeli settlement was based on the strategic and political conception embodied in the famous Allon Plan. Submitted to the Israeli cabinet in a tentative form in July 1967, the plan was approved in June 1968, though only as a settlement strategy and not as a formal political territorial compromise plan. Allon argued that the permanent borders of Israel must be defensible from a strategic point of view and must depend on permanent topographical obstacles that can withstand the onslaught of modern land armies and lend themselves to large-scale retaliatory attacks. Such security borders must also, he argued, be political borders; the border would be political only if Jewish settlements existed along its length. Accordingly, he suggested the annexation of a strip of 10–15 kilometers through the Jordan Valley to the Dead Sea, plus all the Wilderness of Judea and the uninhabited parts of the Hebron Mountains. He also proposed Israeli annexation of the Etzion Block and the Latrun salient. The width of the Jordan strip was later enlarged to 20 kilometers from the river to include the western slopes of the rift valley. Even before the official approval of the Allon settlement plan, Nahal outposts were established (mid-1968). By 1971 the number of settlements in the rift had risen to ten. In 1975 two chains of settlement had been established, one on the rift bed and one on its western slopes. The Allon Road, a patrol road later paved, marked the western border of the settlement area, separating it from the inhabited Arab villages on the desert threshold. True to Labor-Zionist settlement ideology, all Al-

lon settlements are agricultural collectives: 14 moshavim (small holder cooperatives), 6 kibbutzim (communal), and two Nahal outposts and one moshav (collective production and individual households). An urban service center was established but had not been developed. In 1982 the total cultivated area of the rift valley was 34,200 dunams, of which 33,000 dunams were irrigated. A further 24,000 dunams have already been allotted to the existing settlements, and five additional ones are planned for completion by 1986. The settlements use 21.5 million cubic meters of water. Agricultural production is based on production of winter vegetables, bananas, citrus, and flowers. The settlements are planned to contain eighty farm units apiece, fully financed by the World Zionist Organization. The total national investment in the rift settlements, excluding regional infrastructure, is estimated at $100–120 million, $83 million between 1974 and 1983 (see table 14). Despite heavy public investment, the region has been beset by financial difficulties. In 1981–1982 ten moshavim were in deep debt, and consolidation funds had to be provided.

The settler population grew very slowly. In 1975 there were approximately 425 families (1,800 persons). Almost the same number was reported in 1981. The total population in 1983 is estimated at 700 families (including 200 families in the Maaleh Ephraim urban center). The average rate of growth in 1977–1983 was 6.6 percent per annum, or thirty-three families a year. The actual growth is 40 percent of the planned rate envisaged by the Jordan Valley Development Plan of five families per settlement (eighty-five families a year).[1] By the end of 1982, there were 1,402 housing units in the rift region. A comparison of population figures with housing data shows that almost half the units are vacant. The average occupancy ratio is 1.7 units per family.

In light of the information just presented, the growth potential of the rift settlements seems limited.

TABLE 14
EXPENDITURE OF THE WORLD ZIONIST ORGANIZATION ON WEST BANK SETTLEMENTS, 1974–1983
(millions of U.S. dollars)

Region	1974	1975	1976	1977	1978	1979	1980	1981	1982	1983
Rift valley	3.87	3.90	3.11	5.22	3.70	11.15	13.70	12.85	12.65	12.89
Rest of West Bank	1.22	1.20	0.72	5.06	10.14	18.59	23.40	28.20	22.14	21.24
Subtotal	5.09	5.10	3.83	10.28	13.84	29.74	37.10	41.05	34.79	34.13
Jewish National Fund (JNF) land development	0.47	0.36	0.29	0.30	1.20	3.53	3.10	3.27	1.94	1.40
Total	5.56	5.46	4.12	10.67	10.58	33.27	40.20	44.32	36.73	35.53
% spent in rest of West Bank[a]	24	24	19	49	73	63	63	69	64	62

a. Not including JNF land development.
SOURCE: Ministry of Agriculture, Budget Book, 1983.

The *Jordan Valley Development Plan* envisages a 22.5 percent annual increase that will more than double the 1981 population to 970 families by 1986 and 1,450 by 1991.[2] On the basis of the actual growth rate, the 1986 target seems achievable only by 1992, and total Israeli population in the rift will reach 4,500 persons. It should be noted that the total Arab population of the rift valley (the town of Jericho and seven villages) was 28,000 in 1981.

The rift region also includes the south Judea, or south Har Hebron, region. Four settlements and seven Nahal outposts were established in that area. The estimated total number of families in the permanent settlements is 100, not including Nahal outposts. The regional development plan for the Mount Hebron slopes (March 1982) envisaged nineteen settlements with 6,200 families (including one town of 2,500 units), partially on areas within the Green Line. The difficult climatic conditions, lack of cultivable lands, and proximity to Beersheba and the town of Arad do not permit the assumption of a higher growth potential than that of the Jordan Valley.

The low-demand label placed by official Israeli planners on the rift region seems appropriate. The enormous investment in the region and the generous incentives offered to settlers seem to have limited effects. The ideologically motivated settlers required to inhabit this harsh region are in short supply.

The Second Phase: Gush Emunim Settlements

When the October 1973 war broke out, there were seventeen settlements in the West Bank, thirteen in the rift valley, and four in other regions. The trauma of the war, the disengagement negotiations with Egypt and Syria, and the internal Israeli political upheaval put a temporary halt to settlement activities between October 1973 and October 1975.

After the signing of the second disengagement agreement with Egypt, the new Rabin administration embarked on an ambitious settlement program. Settlement activity was officially confined to the Allon Plan regions, but Allon's close associate, Israel Galili, appointed head of the Ministerial Committee on Settlements, interpreted the plan very broadly. In addition, Avraham Ofer, the dovish minister of housing, proposed to thicken Jerusalem by establishing a ring of satellite towns within a radius of fifteen kilometers around the boundaries of greater Jerusalem and took preliminary action to implement his proposal.

The main driving force in the 1975–1977 settlement activity was, however, Gush Emunim. Founded in February 1974 with the objective of settling in "all parts of Eretz Israel," the Gush in June 1974 initiated a series of illegally attempted settlements in central Samaria that were removed by the army. Nevertheless, the Rabin government, joined in 1974 by the militant young faction of the National Religious party and suffering from an endemic personal rivalry between the prime minister and Shimon Peres, the minister of defense, could not resist direct actions by the Gush and gave way. By the time of the May 1977 elections, which brought about the fall of the Rabin government, five Gush Emunìm settlements had been established in the heart of the mountain massif with the unofficial but active support of the minister of defense and the military authorities.

The Gush settlement plan, calling for the establishment of some sixty settlements in the central massif and the western foothills, after the elections of 1977 became the official policy of the World Zionist Organization Department of Settlement. The Drobles Plan (1978, 1980, 1981) articulated the settlement strategy of the Likud and Gush Emunim.

> A dense chain of settlement on the central massif would be a reliable barrier, that would stand in the way of the strong and united [Arab] Eastern Front, threatening Israel. . . . This barrier of settlement would give a sense of security to the rift valley settlers—our first defensive wall in the east—and prevent a situation, whereby they [the rift settlers] would find themselves pressed from East and West by hostile populations. . . . State land and uncultivated land must be seized immediately in order to settle the areas *between* the concentrations of minority population and *around* them, with the objective of reducing to the minimum the possibility for the development of another Arab state in these regions. It would be difficult for the minority population to form a territorial continuity and political unity when it is fragmented by Jewish settlements.[3]

The settlement policy was defined by Drobles thus:

> Settlements should not be isolated. . . . Therefore, near each existing settlement other settlements should be built, so that blocs would be formed. It is conceivable that the expansion of settlements would in some cases result in their natural merger, and an urban settlement would be formed. . . . Most Jewish settlements would be established as rural-communal villages . . . in the coming 5 years [1979–1984 originally, later changed to 1980–1985, and still later to 1981–1986] 12–15 rural and urban settlements should be built each year so that 60–75 additional settlements be established and the

Jewish population would reach 100–120 thousand.[4]

The adoption of the Gush-Likud settlement strategy marked a historic departure from the Labor policy of territorial compromise, which had guided the Zionist movement since 1936, when the first partition plan was proposed by the British Peel Commission. The settlement plan itself was no less revolutionary. The adoption of the *yishuv kehilati* type as the main form of settlement in the West Bank signified a historic departure from the traditional concept of pioneering settlements. Jewish pioneers came to Palestine committed to manual labor and to an agrarian life style in the collective, utopian nuclei of a new and just society. They abhorred the diaspora and the Jewish urban life style. Since the establishment in 1909 of Degania, the first kibbutz, hundreds of kibbutzim, *moshavim*, and *moshavim shitufiim* have been built, with a clear ideological bias against the city and its vices. The older, Gush Emunim, urban middle-class white-collar members were not attracted to that agrarian life style and were not committed to Labor-Zionist ideology. The semiurban, commuting, half-open *yishuv kehilati* was the only form that could attract them. Neither the Gush nor Drobles hid the fact that in the future the *yishuv kehilati* may well be "merged" into an urban settlement and may become a dormitory suburb.

The recognition of the *yishuv kehilati* as a legitimate "pioneering settlement" was not merely an ideological watershed. It meant that Gush Emunim would be eligible for Zionist financial support. All "recognized" types of settlement receive financial aid in the form of grants and very cheap loans for the initial construction of housing and economic infrastructure. The aid continues until the settlement reaches a level of self-sufficiency and is capable of paying back the loans. Many settlements have not reached self-sufficiency even twenty-five years after their establishment. The aid is funneled through a central settlement movement, which coordinates development projects and tends to become a strong economic and political power base.

When the *yishuv kehilati* had been recognized and Gush Emunim had formed its own settlement movement, Amana, the way to a rapid implementation of its settlement plan was clear. Twenty-four settlements were established in 1977–1978, four in 1979, three in 1980, and nine in 1981. Twenty-two were *yishuvim kehilatiim*, and six were urban suburbs; there were twenty-two in the central massif. The shift in strategy and settlement plan can be seen clearly from table 14. The figures reflect only the direct investment of the Zionist Department of Settlement in rural-semiurban settlements under its responsibility. Be-

tween 1978 and 1983, total investment in the Jordan rift was $66.9 million, compared with $123.7 million in the rest of the West Bank. The table also reflects the dramatic increase of investment under Likud. Total investment during the whole decade amounts to $231 million, of which $205.3 million (88.7 percent) was invested between 1978 and 1983. By 1982 there were twenty-one settlements in the central massif region, sixteen *yishuvim kehilatiim*, three nuclei of towns, and two Nahal outposts. The number of families was 1,350, and the number of housing units 2,165, for an occupancy ratio of 1.6 units per family (similar to the ratio in the rift). In 1982 the Matei Binyamin regional council conducted a survey in its nineteen settlements. This survey (see tables 15–17) seems to provide a good indication of the demographic-socioeconomic profile of the settlers in the region. A survey conducted by the Etzion regional council of eight settlements shows the following pattern: of the total population 40 percent are children under eighteen; 41 percent of the labor force commute to work; 36 percent of workers employed on site are engaged in education and public services (21 percent of the total labor force); and 10 percent are employed in agriculture and 15 percent in industry. The tendency of Gush Emunim settlers to be white-collar commuters with higher education and employed in public institutions is evident from these figures.

TABLE 15

DEMOGRAPHIC INDICATORS IN THE MATEI BINYAMIN REGION, 1982

Demographic Indicator	Percentage of Total
Age	
0–18	55.0
18–49	41.0
50+	4.0
No. in family	
2–4	46.7
5–6	43.2
7+	10.1
Years of education	
0–8	0.8
9–12	23.8
13+	65.8
Unknown	9.6
Religious affiliation	
Yes	66.8
No	33.2
Country of origin	
Israeli born	62.0
Europe or North America	27.0
Asia or Africa	11.0

SOURCE: Matei Binyamin Development Plan, table 17.

TABLE 16
PLACE OF WORK OF HEADS OF HOUSEHOLD AND SINGLES IN THE MATEI BINYAMIN REGION, 1982

Place of Work	Percentage of Total
Settlements	29.4
Region	5.4
Jerusalem	34.1
Tel Aviv	13.7
Other	1.4
None (retired)	11.1
Unknown	4.8
Total	100.0

NOTE: Detail does not add to 100.0 because of rounding.
SOURCE: Matei Binyamin Development Plan, tables 20A, B.

The maximum growth rate of the central massif settlement can be estimated by analyzing population figures in two of the oldest settlements, which are also the main centers of Gush Emunim, namely Kfar Etzion and Ofra. The average annual growth rate (families) for Kfar Etzion was 7.7 percent in 1972–1975 and 6.4 percent in 1977–1983. For Ofra the growth rate was 24.4 percent in 1977–1980 and 10.1 percent in 1980–1983 (see table 18). Most other settlements in the massif region show slower rates of growth. The average number of families in 1983 was 45 to 50, ranging from 18 to 100. The sixteen to twenty *yishuvim kehilatiim* in the central massif are planned for 200–300 families. All things being equal, we can expect them to reach 50 percent of their planned capacity (that is, 100–125 families) by 1990, when the total projected population will be 2,000 families, or 8,200 persons.

There are three urban settlements in the massif. Two are *toshava* settlements (Elon Moreh and Maaleh Amos) with a total population in 1983 of 126 families.

TABLE 17
EMPLOYMENT IN SETTLEMENT AND REGION, BY MAIN EMPLOYMENT SECTOR, 1982

Sector	In Settlement	In Region	Outsiders Employed in Settlements
Agriculture	9.6	1.1	0.3
Industry	9.6	19.1	11.3
Commerce and catering	3.5	—	0.8
Financial services	6.6	3.4	10.0
Public institutions	60.6	66.3	58.0
Personal services	7.5	1.1	3.8
Unknown	7.2	3.4	3.9

SOURCE: Matei Binyamin Development Plan, table 19.

TABLE 18
POPULATION IN SELECTED SETTLEMENTS IN THE CENTRAL MASSIF, 1968–1983

	Kfar Etzion		Ofra	
Year	Families	Singles	Families	Singles
1968	10	—	—	—
1972	32	—	—	—
1975	40	—	—	—
1976	42	—	—	—
1977	45	—	39	22
1980	—	—	75	35
1982	—	—	82	11
1983	65	—	100	—

NOTE: Dashes indicate that data are unavailable.
SOURCES: Matei Binyamin Development Plan; Etzion Development Plan; and West Bank Data Base Project.

Assuming a slightly faster growth rate of 15 percent per annum, the number of settlers by the end of the decade in the two *toshavot* would reach about 350 families, or 1,500 persons. The third urban settlement is Kiryat Arba, established in 1968. In late 1977 its population was 1,400 persons (350 families). In 1983 its population reached 750 families, or an average annual growth rate of 13.5 percent. Again, all things being equal, the town will have 2,000 families in 1990.

The total projected population in the entire massif region would therefore reach 2,350 families (10,000 persons) in three urban settlements and 2,000 families (8,200 persons) in sixteen to twenty rural and semiurban settlements, or a total of 18,200 Israelis. If we add up the expected population figures of the rift region, the total Israeli population in the two eastern settlement regions would reach some 5,500 families (23,100 persons) by the end of the decade.

The *scaled-down WZO Plan, 1983–1986* predicts that by 1986 there will be 7,045 families in ninety-nine settlements (four urban, eighty-three rural-semirural, and twelve Nahal outposts) throughout the two regions for an annual growth rate of 47–55 percent.[5] These predictions are grossly exaggerated. Past rates indicate that the settlement target of the WZO would not be reached before the mid-1990s and probably not until later, if at all. The aggressive Gush-Drobles plan of settling "*between* the concentrations of minority population and *around* them" with the objective of creating "a dense chain of settlement on the central massif that would be a reliable barrier" has not been a spectacular success. The planners were the first to realize that it had failed and to identify the reason: the shortage of ideologically motivated settlers who would be ready to leave the metropolitan areas and to live in small, remote, and isolated settlements. Con-

sequently a new strategy was developed, emphasiz-
ing demographic rather than security and ideological
objectives. The new settlement concept initiated a
third phase of Israeli settlement in the West Bank.
Before moving to the third, metropolitan phase, we
should consider Israeli public financing of the settlements, past and planned.

Public Financing

It is difficult to compile accurate public expenditure
data. Official sources do not show separate accounting for civilian expenditure in the territories, the
budget being fully incorporated in general budgets
for Israel. The method adopted by the West Bank Data
Base Project is to use official data on uses and to mul-
tiply it by the official data on cost per unit. According
to West Bank Data Base estimates, the total public
capital investment on civilian projects in the West
Bank for 1967 to 1983 has been $1.5 billion, $750 million under Labor (1967–1973) and $805 million under
Likud (table 19). The heavy military capital investment is, of course, confidential and cannot be estimated.

By comparison, the total capital investment on
civilian projects in the Sinai, totally abandoned, was
$2.2 billion (1967–1981). The breakdown and method
of calculation used were the following.

Construction. By 1984, 12,400 housing units had
been built or were under construction in all types of
settlements at a total cost of nearly $700 million, as
shown in table 20. The total cost figure does not include the cost of land and infrastructure beyond the
boundaries of the settlement.

Industry. The World Zionist Organization estimated the cost per dunam of industrial construction
at $260,000. By 1983, 1,260 dunams had been con-
structed. Investment in industrial infrastructure alone
has thus reached $328 million. This figure does not

TABLE 19
CAPITAL INVESTMENT IN THE WEST BANK, BY SECTOR, 1968–1983
(millions of U.S. dollars)

Housing	690
Industry and production	328
Agriculture	55
Electricity	15
Communications	15
Roads	75
Water	122
Other and unknown	250
Total	1,550

SOURCE: West Bank Data Base Project.

TABLE 20
INVESTMENT IN HOUSING, 1983

Type of Settlement	Units Built	Cost per Unit ($ thousands)	Total Investment ($ thousands)
Urban	7,500	53	397,500
Communal	3,000	58	174,000
Rural	1,900	62	117,800
Total	12,400	—	695,300

SOURCE: West Bank Data Base Project.

include the industrial park at Atarot, which is within
the municipal boundaries of Jerusalem and comprises
some 450 dunams.

Agriculture. Investment in agriculture is calculated from table 14. It is estimated that half the investment in the rift valley and 10 percent of investment in
other regions had been in agriculture, for a total of $55
million.

Electricity. An estimated $15 million has been in-
vested in the electrification of the West Bank, of which
$11 million was invested by the Israel Electric Com-
pany and the rest by the East Jerusalem Electric Company. An estimated 120 kilometers of high-tension
lines have been installed by the Israel Electric Company alone.

Communications. About $15 million has been in-
vested in a telephone network in the region. The development budget has increased during the last few
years, and in 1983 alone an outlay of $13 million is
anticipated for the development of the West Bank telephone network. By 1983 Ariel, Kiryat Arba, Maaleh
Adumim, and Karnei Shomron have been linked.
Ninety settlements already have 1,400 subscribers.
Four exchanges are all in operation, and four more are
being built in Ephrat, Shiloh, Elkanah, and Maaleh
Ephraim.

Roads. We do not have data on the total length of
roads constructed in the West Bank. Between 1979
and 1981, 94 kilometers of roads were constructed. It
is estimated that 200 kilometers of new civilian roads
were constructed between 1967 and 1978. The average
cost per kilometer is $300,000, and it is estimated that
a total of $75 million has been invested in roads.

Water. Investment in the development of water
resources in recent years is shown in table 21. A total
of $68.2 million was invested in water works between
1978 and 1982. We estimate that in the earlier period,
between 1967 and 1977, some $5 million were in-
vested annually, or a total of $55 million, giving a total
investment in water resources of about $123 million
since 1967.

TABLE 21
INVESTMENT IN WATER RESOURCE DEVELOPMENT,
1978–1982
(millions of U.S. dollars)

	1978	1979	1980	1981	1982
Jordan Valley	30.9	5.9	4.47	4.55	2.0
Judea and Samaria	0.5	0.7	4.61	10.34	4.2
Total	31.4	6.6	9.08	14.89	6.2

SOURCE: West Bank Data Base Project.

An additional 20 percent of the total capital investment by the Israeli government is estimated to be needed for additional infrastructure, community services, land acquisition, and unknown items. Table 22 compares existing capital investment and planned investment by 1986. According to the Israeli government planners, the West Bank is ripe for an increased share of private capital investment. Therefore the planners distinguish between national (public) capital investment and other (commercial private) investment. The public participation ratio is estimated at 60 percent of the total investment, or $1,550 billion. The degree of anticipated public participation varies, depending on the branch.

Housing	33 percent
Settlement infrastructure	62 percent
Industry	73 percent
Agriculture	73 percent
Community services	73 percent
Transport, commerce	73 percent
Roads	100 percent
Electricity, water, communications	100 percent
Land acquisition	67 percent

A total capital investment of $2.5 billion means that each year $625 million would be invested, $375 million of which would come from public budgets. Planned annual public expenditure is almost triple the average annual investment in the West Bank between 1977 and 1983. The project is not unfeasible, however, if it is extended to the end of the decade (as it will be in any case because of constraints on implementation) and if it is perceived as the top-priority national project for the 1980s.

Budget allocation on the order of $200 million a year seems reasonable when we consider that the budget of the Ministry of Housing alone (1983–1984) is $815 million. During the 1980s, however, Israel is embarking upon other national projects: the Lavie fighter (conservatively estimated to cost $2.0 billion) and the Dead Sea Canal (costing $1.5 billion). The settlement project, like the whole Israeli economy, depends on the continuation of U.S. aid at least at the

TABLE 22
CAPITAL INVESTMENT, 1968–1983, AND PLANNED INVESTMENT, 1983–1986

	Investment (U.S. $ million)		Number	
	Existing[a]	Planned[b]	Existing[a]	Planned[b]
Housing (units)	690	878	12,500	20,860
Industry (dunams)	328	457	1,260	1,814
Roads (kilometers)	75	125	c.200	395.5
Electricity, water communication (megawatts peak and million cubic meters)	152	104	25 and 126.8	70 and 169.3
Agriculture (dunams)	55	55	55,000	45,000
Community services	—	298	—	—
Settlement infrastructure	—	48	—	—
Land acquisition (dunams)	—	30	—	31,500
Transport, commerce, financial capital investment	—	192	—	—
Unspecified, unforeseen	250	428	—	—
Total	1,550	2,615	—	—

a. 98 settlements.
b. 66 settlements.

SOURCES: Existing investment: table 19; existing units: West Bank Data Base Project and World Zionist Organization, *Development Plan, 1983–1986*; planned investment and units: World Zionist Organization, *Development Plan, 1983–1986*.

TABLE 23
DISTRIBUTION OF THE POPULATION IN THE TEL AVIV CONURBATION, 1961, 1972, AND 1981

	1961		1972		1981	
	Number (thousands)	Percent	Number (thousands)	Percent	Number (thousands)	Percent
Inner city[a]	693	64.6	900	62.7	994	57.2
Suburbs[b]	380	35.4	535	37.3	744	42.8
Total	1,073	100.0	1,435	100.0	1,738	100.0
Percentage of total Israeli population	—	58.0	—	53.4	—	52.3

a. Tel Aviv district.
b. Central district.
SOURCE: Central Bureau of Statistics.

present levels. Changes in U.S. economic support not only would affect public and private investment but also would change the demand patterns on which the new settlement policy is based.

Not all investment in the West Bank is made in addition to investment in Israel. Some of it actually replaces capital investment that would have been made in any case. From a strictly economic point of view, the additional noneconomic-political-ideological public investment is only the component added to normal, economically rational development. Housing units have to be built somewhere; industry and roads must be constructed. The fact that they are built in the West Bank may constitute a political burden but not necessarily an economic one, provided that investment is made according to the laws of supply and demand. Using such a yardstick, we can exclude the investments already made in the rift valley and on the mountain massif, and we can also deduct some $350 million of planned investment. The bulk of the planned expenditure (82.5 percent), however, would be made in the metropolitan areas of Jerusalem and Tel Aviv, where the story is altogether different.

The Third Phase: Suburbia

At the beginning of the 1980s, Israel was well into the suburban era. The trend away from the large cities, especially Tel Aviv, had already begun in the mid-1960s and gathered momentum during the 1970s. The steady move from the inner city to the suburbs is readily apparent in table 23.[6]

The centrifugal trend is evident from the population figures of specific localities within the Tel Aviv conurbation. Out-migration affects not only Tel Aviv–Jaffa but all localities within the inner ring surrounding the inner core. Table 24 shows the centrifugal migration pattern. It should be noted that the localities situated in the outer ring lie within a radius of 24

kilometers, or twenty to forty-five minutes' optimal driving time. Most suburbs are dormitory communities, and residents commute to their places of work and entertainment. The process of residential suburbanization, however, has been accompanied by industrial suburbanization, mainly toward the north and east, along major highways. The largest Israeli industrial plant, the Israel Aviation Industry, employing 20,000 workers, is located 18 kilometers east of Tel Aviv. Industrial dispersal hastened residential suburbanization.

There is almost no need to explain centrifugal

TABLE 24
LOCAL CENTRIFUGAL MIGRATION IN THE TEL AVIV AND CENTRAL DISTRICTS, 1977–1979
(net migration)

	1977	1978	1979	1977–1979
Tel Aviv/Jaffa	−5,767	−4,595	−3,720	−14,082
Inner ring				
Ramat Gan	−1,866	−1,547	−1,526	−4,939
Givatayim	−535	−582	−515	−1,634
Holon	1,979	1,589	1,078	4,646
Bat Yam	553	670	348	1,571
Bnei Brak	−510	−678	−603	−1,791
Total	−379	−548	−1,218	−2,149
Outer ring				
Herzliya	1,544	1,510	1,265	4,319
Kfar Saba	724	535	37	1,296
Ramat HaSharon[a]	1,600	1,500	1,000	4,100
Petah Tikva	701	541	170	1,412
Netanya[a]	3,350	3,700	3,100	10,150
Rehovot	1,559	1,151	699	3,409
Rishon LeZion	3,981	3,173	2,128	9,282
Total	13,459	12,110	8,399	33,968

a. Calculated at half the growth of 1975 to 1977.
SOURCE: Central Bureau of Statistics.

migration. Israeli suburbanization stems from the same socioeconomic factors that cause suburbanization in Western countries. Young middle-class families flee the congested city in search of a one-family or semidetached house with a garden in a semiurban environment at more affordable prices than those prevailing in the inner city. The strong trend in Israel, however, should be understood against the background of the mass immigration waves of the 1950s and early 1960s. Hundreds of thousands of new immigrants were settled in government housing projects in areas that at the time were the outer ring of Tel Aviv. These housing projects were poorly planned, were crowded, and lacked proper community centers. The second and third generation of the new immigrants (many from the Oriental countries) had become affluent by the 1980s, had assimilated middle-class Western values, and had joined their Israeli-born peers in the flight from the instant slums of their parents. A study of land values and apartment prices showed that the price of apartments had risen by more than 60 percent (in real terms) in Tel Aviv (1976–1982), by more than 30 percent in the southern outer ring, and by 50 percent in the northern outer ring. During the same period, salaries rose by only 22 percent. This discrepancy has made apartments within the Tel Aviv conurbation prohibitively expensive.

The same centrifugal trend is discernible in Jerusalem, although its intensity is weaker. The suburban revolution came to Jerusalem only in the 1970s. Until then the city was confined by the armistice lines to its British Mandate site, with additional mass housing projects on the western hills (the only area open for construction). After the Six-Day War, the government decided to build large neighborhoods around the city and thus to "make it indivisible." The new neighborhoods were the Jerusalem version of the suburban dream. They provided larger apartments and a better quality of life, but at the same time they were built as dormitory communities, lacking places of employment and entertainment. The more affluent Jerusalemites, however, sought a real suburban environment. The prohibitive land prices within the city and the very small areas allotted for single houses in the new neighborhoods pushed Jerusalemites to the rural areas along the Jerusalem–Tel Aviv highway. A typical ribbon development of suburb ensued, extending 15 kilometers west of the city limits. Consequently land values in this area, though lower than in the inner city, also became prohibitive. *The strategists of the new settlement phase intend to exploit precisely these centrifugal pulls in both metropolitan areas.*

The stated strategy is to achieve "maximal distribution of a large Jewish population in areas of high settlement importance, with small national input and

in a relatively short time, by the realization of the settlement potential of Judea and Samaria and through its integration in the nation's various systems." The plan is based on two main settlement processes: "*diffused processes* resulting from natural demands" and "*nationally initiated* and supported settlement processes." The settlement plan emphasizes the security and political importance of settlement and suggests an elaborate system of incentives and public capital investment in areas of high settlement priorities in the east and around Arab population centers. This system, however, is mere lip service to the old, ideologically motivated Gush-Drobles plan. The new plan states clearly: "The settlement plan diverts the center of gravity of settlement activity away from the subsidized rural communal villages to the demand forces [pushing] for semi-urban settlements of high quality of life in demand zones." This change in focus, away from the rift and the highlands to the metropolitan areas, aptly redefined as "the high-demand zone," is readily apparent in table 25. In these areas are planned 82½ percent of total investment, the same percentage of new housing construction, almost all industrial plants, and 91.6 percent of total commercial and financial services. The new settlement plan envisages an additional 80,000 settlers in the metropolitan areas by 1986.[7]

It seems strange, at first glance, that those who conceived the "dense barrier" strategy would formulate, three years later, the "diffused processes of demand" concept. Still, it is only a short step from recognizing a commuters' dormitory *yishuv kehilati* as a pioneering settlement to legitimizing suburban sprawl and developers' profiteering as patriotic endeavor.

The World Zionist Organization and the Israeli government did not initiate suburbanization and the quest for a higher standard of living. They just exploit the trend. By identifying it with Zionist values, however, they transformed the entire Israeli value system. From being ideologically motivated and institutionally structured to channel these motivations, Israel has become a Western consumer society pursuing materialistic values. There is nothing wrong in the now legitimized pursuit of an improved standard of living except that in the Israeli case it is mainly based on foreign aid. The evolution of value systems, the restructuring of national institutions, and the redefining of priorities are necessary to adjust to changing realities. In the Israeli case, however, the national ethos—the institutional and symbolic system, structured in the formative period to support and sustain an ideologically motivated society—is not only left intact, but is deliberately reinforced and strengthened, not to instill renewed ideological motivation but to do just the opposite, to facilitate sheer consumerism and

TABLE 25

SETTLEMENT PLAN, 1983–1986

	Rift				Massif				Metropolitan				Total		
	Investment		Persons or units		Investment		Persons or units		Investment		Persons or units		Investment		Persons or units[a]
	U.S. $ million	% of total	No.	% of total	U.S. $ million	% of total	No.	% of total	U.S. $ million	% of total	No.	% of total	U.S. $ million	% of total	Total
Housing	73.0	8.3	1,523	7.3	80.0	9.1	1,720	8.2	725.0	82.6	17,618	84.5	878.0	100.0	20,861
Agriculture	28.8	52.4	412	—	6.2	11.3	89	—	20.0	36.4	292	—	55.0	100.0	793
Industrial estates	4.8	1.4	96	—	12.2	3.4	147	—	338.0	95.2	2,712	—	355.0	100.0	7,120
Local industry	31.6	31.0	422	—	33.4	32.7	268	—	37.0	36.3	201	—	102.0	100.0	1,371
Community services	20.0	6.7	690	—	24.0	8.1	794	—	254.0	85.2	8,471	—	298.0	100.0	9,955
Commerce, financing	6.0	3.1	209	—	10.0	5.2	167	—	176.0	91.7	1,174	—	192.0	100.0	6,411
Total	164.2	8.7	1,942[a]	—	165.5	8.8	1,598[a]	—	1,550.0	82.4	13,815[a]	—	1,880.0	100.0	26,861

NOTE: Dashes indicate data inapplicable.
a. Figures include commuters; totals of all areas/branches therefore add to less than grand total.
b. Including employed in construction.

SOURCE: WZO Plan, 1983–1986.

to exploit it. The consequences of distorted institutional and value systems may prove the heaviest price Israel pays for its West Bank settlement policies. Those who conceived the new strategy, however, are not concerned with such matters. For them the ultimate value is securing the title over the whole of Eretz Israel.

The Likud strategists, unlike their Labor political adversaries, estimate correctly that the decision about the future of the territories will result from domestic political struggles within the Israeli body politic rather than from direct external military or political pressure. Therefore their strategy is aimed at creating *internal* political facts rather than geostrategic facts. Labor continues to advocate an anachronistic strategy of settlement dating back to the "tower and stockade" methods of the 1930s and 1940s: a thin chain of kibbutzim and *moshavim* running through the Jordan Valley is supposed to determine political and military facts. The Likud government knows that this strategy is as relevant in the 1980s as the underground tactics used by the Haganah during the British Mandate. The new Likud settlement strategy is demography oriented. Its objective is to form a strong domestic lobby composed of those who settled in the new suburbs in the West Bank or who have an economic interest in it. It makes no difference whether they settle near the Green Line as long as they are in the occupied territories. The suburban settlers need not hold with the Likud ideology. They will be an effective barrier to any political alternative espousing territorial

compromise simply because they will wish to protect their investment in a higher quality of life.

The suburban settlement plan stands a chance of being carried out with more success than the previous two plans, mainly because settler potential is not limited to the depleted pool of the ideologically motivated or based on an accelerated growth rate of the Jewish population achieved by increased immigration, which is not anticipated. Settler potential depends solely on the continuation of suburbanization, which, all things being equal, is likely to last at least through the 1980s and 1990s. If almost 34,000 people moved to the Tel Aviv outer ring in two years (see table 24), it is not impossible that each year 10,000–15,000 suburbanites would move to new areas situated at the same distances as the outer ring. The main constraints are housing, cheap mortgages, and road construction. The development plan envisages the completion of 17,618 housing units (table 25) in the metropolitan areas (1983–1986), or 4,400 units each year. These figures are much too high. In 1982 the Ministry of Housing approved the construction of 8,000 units throughout the country, 2,000 of which were in the West Bank. Taking into account the average construction time per unit (24.3 months in 1982) and growth in other major development projects, such as the new neighborhoods in Jerusalem, it seems that building starts of 2,500 units a year in public housing plus 500 private build-your-home units are the absolute maximum.

Financial incentives are generous and attractive.

The initial price of an apartment is 15–25 percent lower than across the Green Line. The Land Authority calculates land values at 5 percent of the public assessor's estimate (no loss to the agency, because the land had been "declared"). The Ministry of Housing supplies cheap financing to the construction firm. It guarantees purchase of the apartments if they are not sold. Of 3,741 units that the ministry guaranteed to purchase in the whole of Israel in 1983, 1,007 are in the West Bank.

Financial support in the major urban centers comes to $20,750 per unit for those who lack housing: a $3,000 grant, a $2,250 "unlinked" mortgage (it can be written off because of the inflation), an $11,750 linked mortgage without interest, and for the rest, a mortgage bearing 5.7 percent interest. Many developers advertise that "you can get an apartment in the West Bank with no cash down payment."

Roads are viewed as central to the whole plan, because the road network is crucial for the realization of the demand potential. Roads must allow easy access and fast commuting between the main metropolitan centers and the settlements. The plan calls for the construction of 400 kilometers of roads, 216 kilometers in the metropolitan areas, in four years. Again, this figure is much too high. In 1981, 133 kilometers of roads were completed in the whole of Israel. The major bottlenecks will be removed by 1984–1985, however, namely the major Petah Tikva bypass connecting the trans-Samaria road to the Herzliya–Tel Aviv highway; the Jerusalem–Maaleh Adumin highway; and a new arterial road connecting Ben-Gurion Airport with the northern Jerusalem area as well as Arab town bypasses (see map 2).

Lists of main urban and suburban areas in the Jerusalem and Tel Aviv conurbations and details regarding their size appear in tables 26 and 27.

Conclusion

We may conclude that the interim target of the WZO-Israeli government of 100,000 Israeli settlers in the West Bank will probably not be achieved before the end of the decade. The estimated growth rate is 3,000 families per annum, or 12,500 persons (at 4.2 persons per family). The growth may be faster if construction in the metropolitan area is accelerated. The rift and massif regions will develop very slowly and will reach 5,500 families (23,000 persons) by the end of the decade. The major settler concentration would be in the metropolitan areas (Tel Aviv and Jerusalem), where the Israeli population would reach almost 100,000 persons (23,000 families) by the end of the decade.

The actual and projected growth of the Israeli population is shown in table 28. Map 12 indicates the demographic pattern; map 13 shows the distribution of the Arab population. If population growth and distribution projections are correct, an ethnic map of the West Bank at the end of the decade can be drawn. The West Bank will be divided into four subregions.

TABLE 26

EXISTING AND PLANNED SETTLEMENTS IN THE JERUSALEM METROPOLITAN AREA, 1982

Name of Settlement	Area Existing	Area Planned	Units 1982	Units 1986	Target Units or Families	Families 1982
Maaleh Adumim	13,800	34,000	2,450	4,750	10,000	1,200
Givon Givat Zeev	500	1,500	1,240	1,600	3,000	—
Anatot	200	500	5	45	250	5
Efrat	238	—	330	480	3,000	110[a]
Pesagot	—	200	32	82	150	32
Betar	—	400	5	45	250	5
Har Gilo	—	—	80	180	300	55
Ramat Kidron	—	1,000	—	300	2,000	—
Daniel	150	300	2	60	200	2
Beitunia	—	400	—	—	—	—
Ein Qiniya	—	300	—	—	—	—
Beit El A'B'	—	—	231	222	500	162
Mitzpe Yehuda	—	—	—	300	2,000	
Givat Ehud	—	—	—	200	700	
Hadasha	—	—	50	80	123	—

NOTE: Dashes indicate data unavailable.

a. 1983.

SOURCE: World Zionist Organization, *Development Plan, 1983–1986.*

TABLE 27

EXISTING AND PLANNED SETTLEMENTS IN THE TEL AVIV CONURBATION, 1982

Name of Settlement	Area Existing	Area Planned	Units 1982	Units 1986	Target Units or Families	Families 1982
Ariel	6,000	16,000	1,010	3,410	35,000	330
Kedumim	1,000	2,000	265	400	4,000	170
Karnei Shomron	300	2,200	220	700	2,500	125
Elkanah A–D	2,000	—	200	1,250	3,400	130
Emmanuel	1,670	—	980	4,140	5,000	150[a]
Tzavta	—	—	300	480	2,500	150[a]
Shaarei Tikvah	—	—	70	320	700	—
Cluster of *toshavot* north	—	—	—	3,000	7,450	—
Cluster of *toshavot* south	—	—	—	1,880	5,100	—

NOTE: Dashes indicate data unavailable.

a. 1983.

SOURCE: World Zionist Organization, *Development Plan, 1983–1986.*

1. *The Jordan rift and the eastern slopes of the highlands.* This subregion will be sparsely populated. The number of Israeli settlers will reach 4,500 persons, and the Palestinian population 33,000 (at an average increase of 2 percent per annum). There will be some local ethnic friction resulting from conflicts over water resources. The total area, however, encompassing some 1.5 million dunams, will be mainly a military training ground and defense installation zone.

2. *The mountain massif.* A narrow strip 100 kilometers long and 10–20 kilometers wide along the Jerusalem-Nablus-Jenin and Bethlehem-Hebron highways will be densely populated by 500,000–550,000 Palestinians and will be heavily built up. In that area some 20,000 Israeli settlers will be scattered in ten to twenty-five permanent settlements. The area will be dissected by new east-west roads and by bypasses that will connect Israeli settlements. Although the demographic presence of the Israelis will be minuscule (3.5 percent), their physical presence will be substantial. The land seized for settlement construction is meant to be sufficient for the maximal expansion of the sites; all available natural resources will be monopolized by the settlers, and a nonsettler Israeli presence will be created by developing parks, nature reserves, archaeological sites, grazing grounds, military installations, and paramilitary outposts. The ethnic friction will be intense because the settlements in that region will remain the stronghold of Israeli zealots, who will act as the only legitimate authority in the area. Palestinian resistance will provoke acts of vigilantism. A glimpse of the future ethnic relations in that area

is provided by the existing tension in the Hebron area, where a community of Israeli zealots (Kiryat Arba) numbering 3,500 persons terrorizes and controls a population of 70,000 Palestinians.

TABLE 28

JEWISH POPULATION IN THE WEST BANK, ACTUAL AND PROJECTED, 1972–1990

	Jewish Population
Actual	
1972	1,182
1973	1,514
1974	2,019
1975	2,581
1976	3,176
1977	5,023
1978	7,361
1979	10,001
1980	12,424
1981	16,119
1982	21,000
1983	27,500
Projected	
1984	40,000
1985	52,500
1986	65,000
1987	77,500
1988	90,000
1989	102,500
1990	115,000

SOURCE: Actual population figures are from the Central Bureau of Statistics; projected figures are the author's estimates.

TABLE 29

ETHNIC COMPOSITION OF JERUSALEM METROPOLITAN AREA, 1981 AND 1991

(thousands)

	Jews		Arabs		Total		% Jews		% Arabs	
	1981	1991	1981	1991	1981	1991	1981	1991	1981	1991
Within municipal boundary	298	335	117	146	415	481	72.3	70.2	27.7	29.8
Periphery within Green Line	15	18	3	4	18	22				
15-kilometer radius in West Bank	4	25[a]	128	150	132	175	3.0	14.3	97.0	85.7
Total	317	378	248	300	565	678	56.1	55.8	43.9	44.2

a. Ninety percent of the settlers originate in Jerusalem.

SOURCES: 1981 data from Central Bureau of Statistics; predictions for 1991 are the author's.

3. *The Jerusalem metropolitan area.* This area, encompassing roughly half a million dunams within a radius of 15 kilometers from Jerusalem on both sides of the Green Line, had a total population of 565,000 persons in 1981. Its ethnic composition, existing and projected, is shown in table 29. There will be a small Jewish majority (56 percent), but most of the Jewish population will remain in West Jerusalem, and therefore the countryside will be overwhelmingly Arab (86 percent).

The massive Israeli housing construction will erase the old demarcation line but will create scores of new demarcation line between homogeneous Jewish and Arab localities, a tribal map of alienated islands. The spread of Jewish localities will expand points of friction and will make alienation more noticeable to increasing numbers of Jews and Arabs. Interaction will be tenuous. The deep-seated animosity and mutual sense of insecurity will create a very high level of perceived threat, resulting in total dichotomization. The main meeting points will be in the marketplaces, factories, and building sites. Encounters in these places will be characterized by the clear hierarchy that prevails where the Jews are dominant and the Arabs subservient. The metro-

politan area will, indeed, function as one unit only in the economic sphere. In all other spheres, it will function as a dual system. Jewish and Arab localities in close proximity will be subject to separate and unequal conditions: administrative, political, judicial, economic, ecological, infrastructural, and social.

Wherever they settle, the Jews carry the Israeli administrative, political, and welfare state system. They build their own high-level physical infrastructure and enjoy the generous subsidies that attracted them to the West Bank. Imbued with nationalistic pathos, they will monopolize the environment. The Arabs will remain subject to the norms of the military government, disfranchised and discriminated against even when officially annexed to Israel (like the East Jerusalem Palestinian community), excluded from the benefits of the Israeli welfare system even when they are full-time employees in Israeli enterprises, lacking proper physical infrastructure, fragmented and harassed, and powerless to shape their future or to resist further encroachment.

This hierarchy of superiors and inferiors, a "horse and rider" coexistence, will prevail through-

TABLE 30

ETHNIC COMPOSITION OF TEL AVIV CONURBATION, NORTHEAST SECTOR, 1983 AND 1991

(thousands)

	Jews		Arabs		Total		% Jews		% Arabs	
	1983	1991	1983	1991	1983	1991	1983	1991	1983	1991
Within Green Line	65	75	100	122	165	197	39.4	38.1	60.6	61.9
Within West Bank	4	70	128	150	132	220	3.0	31.8	97.0	68.2
Total	69	145	228	272	297	417	23.2	34.8	76.8	65.2

SOURCES: 1983 data from Central Bureau of Statistics; 1991 predictions are the author's.

out greater Israel, but its ugly significance will be truly perceived only in the metropolitan patchwork of tribal enclaves.

4. *The Tel Aviv conurbation.* The vast Tel Aviv metropolitan area stretches along the Mediterranean coast in a strip 60 kilometers long and 20 kilometers wide and contains more than half the Israeli population and three of every five Israeli industrial plants. That vast, almost homogeneous Jewish area will be affected little by the incorporation of the Kfar Saba–Ariel salient, where most Jewish settlement will take place. In the northeastern part of the Tel Aviv conurbation, however, from Rosh Ha'ayin in the south to halfway between Tul Karm and Netanya in the north, an ethnic patchwork similar to that of the Jerusalem area is being created. As we can see from table 30, in that area a sizable Israeli Arab population is situated within the Green Line. With the integration of the Tul Karm (West Bank) subdistrict, the Arab population on both sides of

the Green Line will form an integrated community outnumbering the Jewish population on both sides of the Green Line. Potential ethnic friction in that sector, though probably smaller than in Jerusalem, should not be overlooked.

Notes

1. *Jordan Valley Development Plan* (1982), sec. 3/7.
2. Ibid.
3. Matitiahn Drobles, *Settlement in Judea and Samaria,* WZO, Jerusalem, September 1980, p. 3 (emphasis added).
4. Ibid., pp. 3–4.
5. WZO *Plan, 1983–1986*, tables 4B, 4C.
6. Data on suburbia are based on data included in Annette Hochstein, *Metropolitan Links between Israel and the West Bank* (Jerusalem: WBDB Project, July 1983).
7. WZO *Plan, 1983–1986*, secs. 1.1, 2.2.1.1 (emphasis added).

7

A Turning Point?

The data on the West Bank and Gaza compiled in our project strongly suggest that the processes set in motion in 1967 and accelerated in recent years have created social, economic, and political interactions between Israel and the territories that have assumed quasi permanence. Moreover, we can now say with some assurance that we have begun a new chapter in the history of Palestine. In the 101st year since the beginning of the Zionist enterprise, in the thirty-sixth year since the establishment of the state of Israel, the Zionist movement has achieved its maximum territorial goal: control over the entire area of Mandatory Palestine.

Less dramatically, we might define the situation in the following fashion: the political, military, socioeconomic, and psychological processes now working toward the total annexation of the West Bank and the Gaza Strip outweigh those that work against it. The gap between the contending forces will ultimately permit the complete integration of the occupied territories. Considered statistically, those processes do not yet appear to have reached the point of no return. When we consider the dynamics of all the forces as well as the time element, however, we can see that the critical point has passed.

The 1948 war gave birth to the state of Israel; however, the continuing war of liberation, in the sense that it establishes borders reflecting national aspirations, has only now been concluded. That perception is not limited to the hypernationalist groups advocating greater Israel. It is shared by more moderate elements within the Israeli body politic. For a short period after the war in 1967, Israeli leaders were in doubt about what to do with the territories and even offered to withdraw from them in return for peace. Very quickly, however, a new conception took over, which interpreted the Six-Day War as a direct extension of the war of liberation, taking care of "unfinished business." The Israeli national consensus, explicitly or implicitly, views the nineteen years during which Palestine was divided as a stage in the realiza-

tion of national aspirations that can be seen as an extension of prestate Zionist activity.

The significance of that ultimate achievement of Zionist aspirations, more than territorial, is that the Palestinian problem has now been internalized. Henceforth the major responsibility for the fate of the Palestinians falls upon Israel. An observer may, of course, cling to the accepted view that the Palestinian problem is an external matter to be dealt with by the "Arab states," an approach that might have been suitable with regard to the refugees of 1948 and the small Israeli Arab minority. Now, however, more than 2 million Arabs live under Israeli rule—half of all the people who identify themselves as members the Palestinian nation—and they cannot be ignored. If in fact the territorial goals of Zionism have been achieved, then the Palestinians have become a permanent minority, 38 percent of the population of the territorial entity ruled by Israel. In other words, what political scientists call a dual society, or in (inappropriate) political jargon a "binational state," is no longer a vision of the future but an actuality.

These far-reaching conclusions are based on an examination of the three principal circles of influence affecting the process: the Israelis, the Americans, and the Arabs and the Palestinians.

The Israelis

For many outsiders the term "settlement" conjures up an image of huts strewn on a wind-swept barren hill with a group of bearded religious zealots gathered around an Israeli flag. The settlement phase initiated by ideologically motivated groups mobilized by Gush Emunim, however, is now over. The typical settler of the 1980s is a figure well known throughout the Western world: the suburbanite. The man who wants to escape his cramped apartment in the stifling, polluted center city and to make his dreams of a home of his own with a bit of lawn come true is not guided by nationalistic ideology. In his social and economic characteristics, he is similar to the average Labor voter. The main demand of these settlers is to be not more than a half-hour's drive from their places of work and entertainment centers.

The officials responsible for settlements are well aware of the needs of *Homo suburbanus*; they are concentrating most of their efforts on the region termed (officially) "the area of high demand"—that is, a ring of settlements encircling Jerusalem and Tel Aviv. Their efforts are made at the expense of investments in the development of more distant areas where the settlers are more ideologically motivated, whether in the Jordan Valley or in the Gush Emunim settlements (or, for that matter, in the Negev and the Galilee in Israel itself).

The Likud government has implemented a settlement policy completely different from that of Labor. The difference does not lie only in the policy of building settlements in areas heavily populated by Arabs, which is an abomination to Labor; the major innovation has been aimed at creating internal political facts, not geostrategic facts. The Likud estimated correctly that the decision about the future of the territories would result from domestic political struggles within the state of Israel rather than from direct external military or political pressure.

The Likud government formed a domestic lobby composed of those who settled in the new cities and suburbs on the West Bank or who have an economic interest in the region. It makes no difference whether they settle near the Green Line, as long as they are in the occupied territories. Knowing that the percentage of the floating vote in Israel is small, the Likud estimates that 100,000 people, representing four or five marginal seats in the Knesset, would be an effective barrier to any political alternative espousing the principle of territorial compromise. The suburban settlers need not hold with the Likud ideology; they simply wish to protect their investment and the higher quality of life they will have attained.

Labor continues to represent an anachronistic strategy of settlement, dating back to the tower-and-stockade methods of the 1930s and 1940s. A thin chain of kibbutzim and *moshavim* running through the Jordan Valley, where the total number of settlers is smaller than in a single neighborhood of one of the cities on the West Bank, is supposed to determine political and military facts and to guarantee secure borders for Israel.

The strategy is as relevant to the reality of the 1980s as the "flying columns" mobilized by the Haganah during the Arab revolt. The creation of the new settlement lobby begun by the Begin administration was supposed to take three or four years. The necessary resources are people, land, the technical capacity to implement the plan, and financing. We have seen that this project can be carried out, provided that there is enough time to do so.

The chances that an internal political force will halt the process of annexation in the post-Begin era seem as slim as they were before his resignation. The Likud government is committed to his legacy; in the event that a Labor-led coalition is formed or a Labor-Center coalition wins national elections, we may expect a change in style—an avoidance of extreme religious and historical claims—but not in substance. In fact, a Labor victory would probably set off a new wave of settlers who would insist on going to the West Bank for ideological reasons. In view of the momentum for establishing the settlements and the pressure that would arise if a new government tried to stop them, the magic formula of "a freeze on settlements and territorial compromise," which many think is the key to renewed peace efforts, would not produce practical results, even if it were finally uttered by a more moderate government.

If and when the Jordanians and Palestinians retract their refusal to participate in negotiations, the talks may well lead nowhere. The most recent moderate Labor formula for a territorial compromise proposes to annex 40 percent of the territories along with 40 percent of their inhabitants. More generous offers were made to King Hussein by Labor governments in the past, and Hussein refused them categorically. Even if both the Labor government and the Jordanians tried to be more flexible, as it is certainly to be hoped they will, they would encounter grave obstacles. The dispute over the future of the West Bank among politicians and in the Israeli press has obscured a broad national consensus on the day-to-day transformation of the territories. Among those who are ideologically motivated, the old Zionist ethos is still powerful. Others, who lack ideological motivation, have strong materialistic motives. The morally troubling questions that have arisen since the Israeli occupation, the reports of violence, of arbitrary administrative actions, and of the dual system of law and personal status are, for the most part, swallowed up in a sea of indifference.

The continuing entanglement in Lebanon exhausts national energies and overshadows the West Bank issue. Dovish groups have pinned their hopes on the outside world, primarily the United States, to exert pressure and halt the annexation. Their sense of dependence on the United States has shown that they do not believe that they can consolidate enough power domestically to reverse the process. Few seem to believe that their prospects are greatly changed by Begin's resignation.

Under the Likud government during the last six years, physical, juridical, and administrative facts have been created at a dizzying pace. The turning point that led directly to annexation, however, took place not in 1977 but rather ten years earlier. On the seventh day of the Six-Day War, the Labor government perceived its rule over the West Bank as temporary and proclaimed its willingness for territorial compromise. Labor also went on, however, to establish the legal basis and physical facilities for the settlements that were indispensable to Ariel Sharon in 1979 when he inaugurated the extensive suburbanization of the West Bank. The trans-Samaria and Allon highways, Kiryat Arba, Ariel, Maaleh Adumin, Kadum, and Ofra were planned and largely built under the Labor government (as of course were the Jordan Valley settlements). The definition of Israeli settlements as "temporary" and the official willingness to "return" populated lands were little more than an attempt by Labor to paper over deep ideological contradictions.

The Americans

Those attuned to the thinking of the American foreign policy establishment and the communications industry on its periphery realize that substantial change in the Palestinian problem and the fate of the territories has been taking place. Since 1967 the degree of urgency attributed by American foreign policy makers to the Palestinian problem has shifted up and down. For sixteen years it has consumed a disproportionate share of intellectual and financial resources and especially time, because it was of importance to each of the rival schools of American foreign policy—roughly speaking, the *Realpolitik* school and the ethical school.

Members of the former school saw failure to find a solution to the problem as a major cause of the endemic instability of the Middle East and held that the instability, in turn, enabled the Soviet Union to gain a foothold there. They also believed that America's energy supply was linked to the Palestinian problem and that failure to solve it jeopardized vital American relations with the great petroleum suppliers. The ethical school, however, saw the conquest of the West Bank and the Gaza Strip as an injustice that had to be corrected by obtaining the right of self-determination for a people deprived of sovereignty. No matter the school to which it subscribed, every new American administration awarded the highest priority to the problem of the territories.

American freedom of action in dealing with the Palestinian problem, however, has been limited because of Israel's solid position in public opinion and consequently in both houses of Congress. Public opinion favorable to Israel has depended to a great extent on the Jewish lobby and the Jewish vote; how-ever, Israel also possesses strong support among non-Jewish groups that view Israel as a bastion of democracy and as an island of Western civilization in a sea of savagery. Masked pro-Arab and anti-Semitic tendencies are counterbalanced by contempt for the backward Orientals. The special relations between the United States and Israel are so intimate that some people claim the state of Israel and its problems are more important to Washington than the state of Iowa and its problems. Because of those special relations and because of unforeseen changes in the Middle East, lack of leadership, sloppy thinking, and especially the inability to exert effective pressure on the ruling powers within Israel and with its Arab rivals, the enormous diplomatic resources invested by the Americans in the Palestinian problem have borne no fruit.

The Reagan administration, which is both conservative and drawn to *Realpolitik*, has replaced the well-meaning Carter administration. Reagan pays far more attention to global and strategic considerations than to ethical considerations such as human rights. Israel's importance as a strategic asset has increased in direct proportion to the weakening of the Arabs and the collapse of the Organization of Petroleum Exporting Countries (OPEC). Alexander Haig gave tacit approval to Israel on the eve of the war in Lebanon because he believed that the war would strengthen America's position at the expense of the Soviet Union and its Syrian client. When the true aim of the war became clear and the new Palestinian tragedy was revealed in its full horror, the United States attempted to clear itself of all blame by publishing the Reagan initiative. The initiative was ill timed, and it was clear from the start that its chances of success were very slight, at least as long as the crisis in Lebanon lasted. Hussein's refusal to accept the initiative officially, after months of floating optimistic rumors, relieved the administration of the necessity of persisting in its plans. Meeting with failure everywhere, the United States desperately needed success. That was supplied by Israel in the form of an agreement with Lebanon worked out by the secretary of state, George Shultz.

Suddenly the political skies cleared, and relations between the two states became friendly again. Officials in Washington have begun to distinguish between the "global interests" of the United States in the region and "the problem of the West Bank and Gaza," which does not, they believe, pose an immediate threat to American interests. Annexation, they say, is a *fait accompli* in any case; although it damages Israel's image as a liberal democracy and thus embarrasses the Americans, Israel is a pariah anyway. Reports on incidents in the territories do not further Israel's international isolation, they claim, because Israel could hardly be more isolated. There is also a growing feeling that the West Bank is an internal Israeli problem.

Fatigue underlies all these arguments. The Americans are sick and tired of the conflict. They are behaving just as people do in private life after they have tried to solve a problem without success: they persuade themselves that it is actually not important.

The United States will doubtless continue to show concern for the territories, expressed as in President Reagan's recent statements, but increasingly the issue of the settlements will become the province of do-gooders and bleeding hearts; the constituency that has been helpless to prevent mass murder in Central America will probably be even less effective with regard to a conflict in which it is much harder to tell the good guys from the villains.

Anyone who looks forward to or fears an imposed settlement is waiting in vain. In view of the present atmosphere in Washington, the chances that the Americans will act more firmly now than they have during the past sixteen years are extremely slim.

The Arab-Palestinian Factor

Whoever wishes to reckon the true power of what is called the Arab world and its willingness to act in behalf of the Palestinian cause should take a good look at the events of recent months: the reaction of the Arab states, including Syria and Libya, to the Palestinians' appeals for help last summer when they were besieged in Beirut; the Arab states' reluctance to accept the evacuees; their indifference to the fate of hundreds of thousands of Palestinian refugees in Lebanon; their inability to agree on any statement on any substantive issue, from the Reagan initiative to the Israeli-Lebanese agreement or even the war between Iran and Iraq. The weakness of the Arab world, the dimensions of which were revealed by Fouad Ajami years ago, reached an unprecedented low in 1983. Hidden behind the impressive facade of OPEC and its petrodollars was a rather wretched reality, which was manifest to all observers when the petroleum cartel collapsed. Nonetheless, there are those who stubbornly maintain the myth of Arab power to use it for their own ends. Not least among them is the government of Israel.

Even in the glorious days of Nasser's pan-Arabism, devotion to the Palestinian cause was a limited devotion. Everyone paid lip service but acted only when it suited the interests of the Arab regimes. Now, in addition to the weakness of the Arab world, we see only fatigue and a feeling of impotence in Arabs' reaction to the Palestinian problem. The Arab states took on responsibility for the fate of the Palestinians forty-five years ago when the Palestinian leadership collapsed after the failure of the Arab revolt of 1936–1939. Many Arabs now have the feeling, especially in the so-called moderate states, that they have done what they could and that they can no longer afford to make sacrifices on the altar of the "Palestinian problem." They continue to pay lip service, but they find justification for their indifference and fatigue in the extremist and ill-considered actions of the Palestinian leaders.

The acts of the PLO, with all its various factions, both before and after the war in Lebanon can only be called self-destructive. That collective character trait is far from new and has frequently been manifest in the history of the Palestinian national movement. Trapped in the rejection of any short-term settlement if it contradicts their ultimate goal, convinced that people must not compromise on matters of principle in a just cause, the Palestinians have waged a hopeless life-or-death struggle with the Zionist movement. They were contemptuous of Zionism until it was too late, but even then they did not cease to believe that they would succeed in exterminating it by force. Thus they brought disaster upon themselves.

The trait of self-destruction was particularly conspicuous both before the Lebanese war and during it. The attempt by the PLO to develop an independent military force that it could use against Israel in southern Lebanon was hopeless from the start. The very attempt to create such a force endangered the active and powerful national center that could have been developed in Beirut and that could only exist in Lebanon because of the particular conditions prevailing in that country. The provocation in southern Lebanon offered Begin and Sharon an excuse to attack the national center in Beirut, to scatter its activists to the four winds, and to destroy their centers of research and thought. All the efforts that were invested in maintaining a people's militia among the inhabitants of the refugee camps went down the drain. The PLO leaders had failed to inspire a popular uprising in the occupied territories during the 1960s and the 1970s, and in similar fashion they also failed among the Palestinians in southern Lebanon. The loss of their headquarters in Beirut set the Palestinian people back twenty years and once again turned them into a flock of refugees subject to the mastery of the states that gave them asylum, serving as pawns in the masters' hands.

After the tragedy in Beirut was over, the PLO could still have rescued the remnant of its political strength. The sympathy that the Palestinians won after the Israeli bombardments and the remorse of the United States for its silent support of the war in Lebanon produced the Reagan initiative, which was an opportunity to convert the military debacle into a political victory. The life ring offered to the PLO was rejected, however, with the excuse that acceptance was impossible because of internal disagreement.

The somnambulant policies of the leaders of the PLO are expressed in practically everything that happens in the occupied territories. The PLO refuses to realize that the annexation of the territories is approaching the point of no return. If it does not adopt realistic policies, it will lose not only the Palestinians' land but also its inhabitants. The significance of the physical facts that have been created in the territories was the principal reason for King Hussein's willingness to pursue the Reagan initiative. Those facts have not made the PLO budge from its position. When some moderates had the courage to warn against the impending disaster, they were either silenced or assassinated. The Palestinian population of the territories has been neutralized because both Israel and the PLO have joined forces to destroy any chance for the growth of local political leadership. The radicals managed to torpedo every attempt to adopt realistic positions. The violent clashes that have recently taken place between the nationalistic students and the Muslim Brotherhood offer yet another sign of the feelings of frustration and lack of direction that reign in the territories, and the bloody skirmishes last summer between the Fatah factions in the Bekaa Valley complete the picture.

In mid-1983 the PLO's relevance steadily decreased. Its leaders will continue to fly from country to country in their executive jets. The Arab states will continue to give the PLO heavy financial support. The PLO will also continue to be the darling of some radicals in Israel and many in the rest of the world; the Palestinian issue will not cease to be a shibboleth identifying individuals as grouped with either the "reactionary" or the "radical" camps, and the debate about whether the PLO has become more moderate and whether it should be recognized will continue. Perhaps a new wave of international terror will begin—or perhaps, alternatively, the PLO will decide to change course and join in the search for a political solution. None of these choices, however, will exert much influence on events in the West Bank and the Gaza Strip, on international politics, on relations between the superpowers, or on political developments within the region.

With all its factional quarrels, cut off from reality in its homeland, manipulated by the Arab regimes for their own ends, and trapped in its unrealistic conceptions, the PLO will have little influence on the course of events. Twice in their history the Palestinians made a heroic effort to wage war alone against their Zionist enemies: between 1936 and 1939 against both the British and the Jewish *yishuv* and in 1947 against the embryonic state. Both efforts ended in tragedy, after which the Palestinians were forced to consign their

fate to their "sister Arab states." The third attempt, the Lebanese war, is apparently also the last.

The Palestinian national entity was defeated and has become a phantom, but that phantom will continue to pursue its victors and the whole world. Followers of the Jabotinsky-Begin ideology and those who admire Sharon and Eitan will discover, to their surprise, that phantoms can be more dangerous than physical beings. Shadows cannot be beaten with sticks. The phantoms will rise from their graves, and Palestinian nationalism, which some have tried to destroy physically and others have tried to destroy conceptually, will give no respite. Absolute victories of such magnitude were possible in other eras. Many national and ethnic groups have been repressed, scattered, and made to disappear, but during their prolonged struggle with Zionism, the Palestinians have formed themselves into a solid mass that will not disintegrate. Near the turn of the twenty-first century, we cannot expect the enlightened world, cynical as it may be, to reconcile itself to the disappearance of the Palestinian nation. Moreover, after they acquire more perspective on recent history, many Israelis will come to understand that, notwithstanding the intransigence of the PLO, the Palestinians were scattered to the winds not because they were wicked murderers but for the simple and cruel reason that they stood in the way. The feeling among Israelis that this reason is simply not sufficient and that their victory was too great will increasingly come to haunt them.

The Dilemma

For all practical purposes the annexation of the West Bank and the Gaza Strip now seems only a matter of time. Theoretically the process might be "reversible," but a realistic estimate of the forces at work for annexation as against those that oppose it invites the conclusion that for the foreseeable future all of Palestine will be ruled by an Israeli government, that the Israeli-Palestinian conflict has therefore become an internal, ethnic conflict, and that Israel is now a dual society.

One difficulty in realizing the virtual permanence of the present situation is that there is no fixed determination of "annexation." Indeed, no one is interested in finding one. Many observers believe that only the formal application of Israeli law to the territories—which has not yet taken place—would be a sure sign of annexation. But the prevailing laws that have been worked out by the Israelis show every sign of being permanent. To refrain from formally applying Israeli law is merely to erect a smoke screen that serves the interests of both the advocates of annexation and their opponents. The advocates know that formal annexation would oblige them to deal with the question of the permanent status of the Palestinians;

the opponents are interested in retaining the illusion of nonannexation, since it allows them to cling to another illusion—that the options remain open. The indifferent majority could not care less.

Defining the system in force in the territories is not, however, a theoretical matter. Misunderstanding the true significance of the situation could allow the development of a regime ominously similar to that of South Africa. The political realities of Palestine in the 1980s are reminiscent of what was called "*Herrenvolk* democracy." In such a system the minority (sometimes even the majority) is disfranchised and deprived of basic civil rights; in contrast, the ruling group enjoys all the attributes of democracy. Such a system should not be confused with a dictatorship. On the contrary, the dominant ethnic group plays by all the rules of democratic freedom, but only that group can benefit from them. Israel annexed East Jerusalem and the Golan Heights, for example, without automatically granting voting rights to their residents. Until now it has been possible to justify this situation as part of a "military occupation" that temporarily deprives the occupied citizens of their political rights until the signing of a peace treaty. Now the "temporary" occupation merely camouflages the consolidation of a hierarchy of superiors and inferiors.

In just two years a generation of Israelis and Palestinians will come of age who were born after 1967. These young people have known only the present reality. The new reality makes the present division between hawks and doves over the issue of partition or integrity of Palestine an anachronism. Now, faced with prospect of ruling over more than a million Arabs who will not have full democratic rights, both sides must offer realistic answers to a different question: Is Israel to be a Jewish state or a democratic one?

That question, which was hypothetical until now, has become an immediate dilemma. The doves must contend with the situation against which they warned but which they were powerless to prevent. The hawks must contend with the reality for which they worked while ignoring its unbearably heavy cost. In grappling with the new situation, hawks and doves might discover, to their surprise, that they are in the same camp. Some doves support territorial compromise not because of their liberal views but because they are afraid of the Arabs and are xenophobic. More than a few hawks are seriously worried that the Zionist dream will become a nightmare that will destroy the character of the state.

The dilemmas that Israel faces are not limited to policy decisions regarding the territories but are more fundamental. They pose the deep question whether the entire Zionist conception, which became fossilized somewhere between 1936 and 1948, can be made to fit the reality that has now emerged. It seems that the institutional, party, educational, and symbolic systems of Israel must all be reevaluated. A new equilibrium between nationalistic objectives and humanistic values must be found. Zionism cannot escape the fate of other great liberating philosophies. Its failure to adjust to changing realities may turn it into a dark force.

Maps

Sources of Information

Map 1: Chapter 3, notes 1 and 2, this volume.

Map 2: Chapter 3, note 5, this volume.

Map 3: Ministry of the Interior, Outline Area Plan Change 1/82 to Area Plan RJ5, 1982.

Map 4: Chapter 3, notes 6 and 11, this volume.

Map 5: *Master Plan and Development Plan for Settlement in Samaria and Judaea* (Jerusalem: World Zionist Organization, Ministry of Agriculture, April 1983), map no. 1.

Map 6: Ibid., map no. 2.

Map 7: Maps attached to *Military Orders 783, 982* as amended.

Map 8: Survey of Israel, Ordinance Survey maps, State of Israel, Tel Aviv; David Kahan, "Agriculture and Water in the West Bank and Gaza," mimeographed (Jerusalem: West Bank Data Base Project, 1983), pp. 20–24, tables 8 and 9.

Map 9: Jewish regional council boundary—*Military Orders 783, 982* as amended; military government subdistrict boundary—Survey of Israel, Administrative Division, February 1981.

Maps 10, 11, 12, and 13: West Bank Data Base Project.

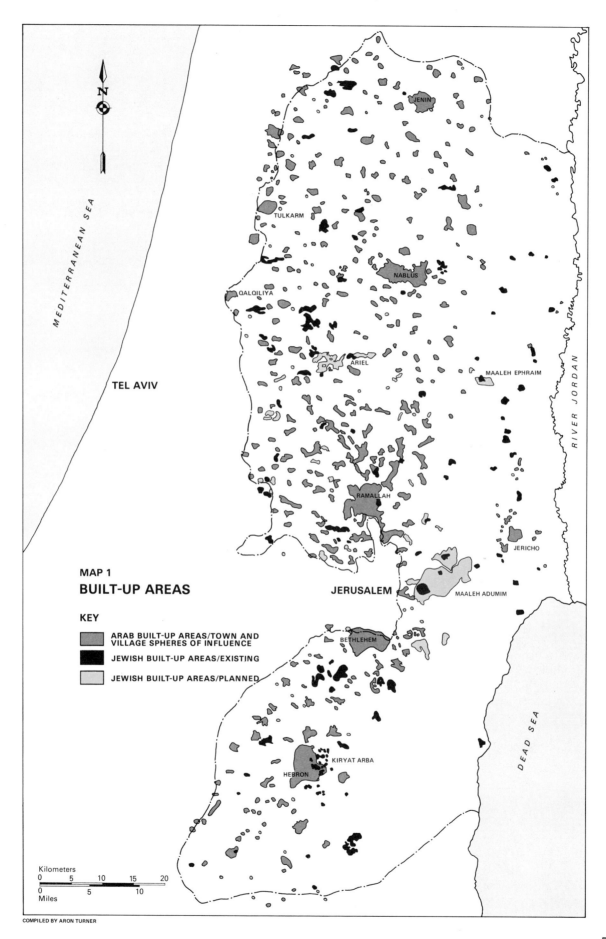

N

MEDITERRANEAN SEA

TEL AVIV

JENIN

TULKARM

NABLUS

QALQILIYA

ARIEL

MAALEH EPHRAIM

RIVER JORDAN

MAP 1

BUILT-UP AREAS

RAMALLAH

JERICHO

JERUSALEM

MAALEH ADUMIM

KEY

ARAB BUILT-UP AREAS/TOWN AND
VILLAGE SPHERES OF INFLUENCE

JEWISH BUILT-UP AREAS/EXISTING

JEWISH BUILT-UP AREAS/PLANNED

BETHLEHEM

DEAD SEA

KIRYAT ARBA

HEBRON

Kilometers
0   5   10   15   20

0   5   10
Miles

COMPILED BY ARON TURNER

73

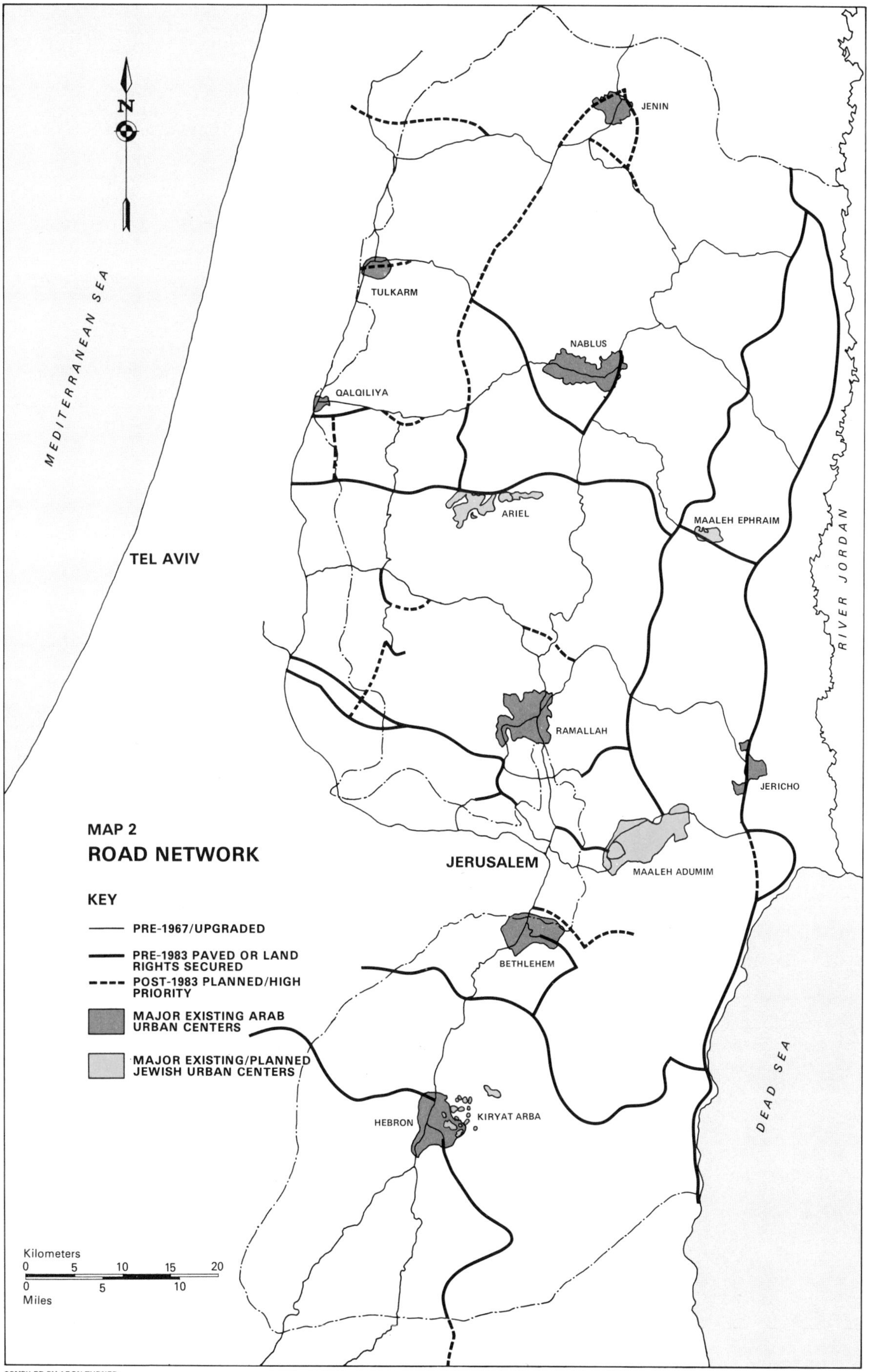
MAP 2
ROAD NETWORK
KEY
PRE-1967/UPGRADED
PRE-1983 PAVED OR LAND RIGHTS SECURED
POST-1983 PLANNED/HIGH PRIORITY
MAJOR EXISTING ARAB URBAN CENTERS
MAJOR EXISTING/PLANNED JEWISH URBAN CENTERS
N
MEDITERRANEAN SEA
TEL AVIV
JENIN
TULKARM
NABLUS
QALQILIYA
ARIEL
MAALEH EPHRAIM
RIVER JORDAN
RAMALLAH
JERICHO
JERUSALEM
MAALEH ADUMIM
BETHLEHEM
DEAD SEA
HEBRON
KIRYAT ARBA
Kilometers
0 5 10 15 20
0 5 10
Miles

COMPILED BY ARON TURNER

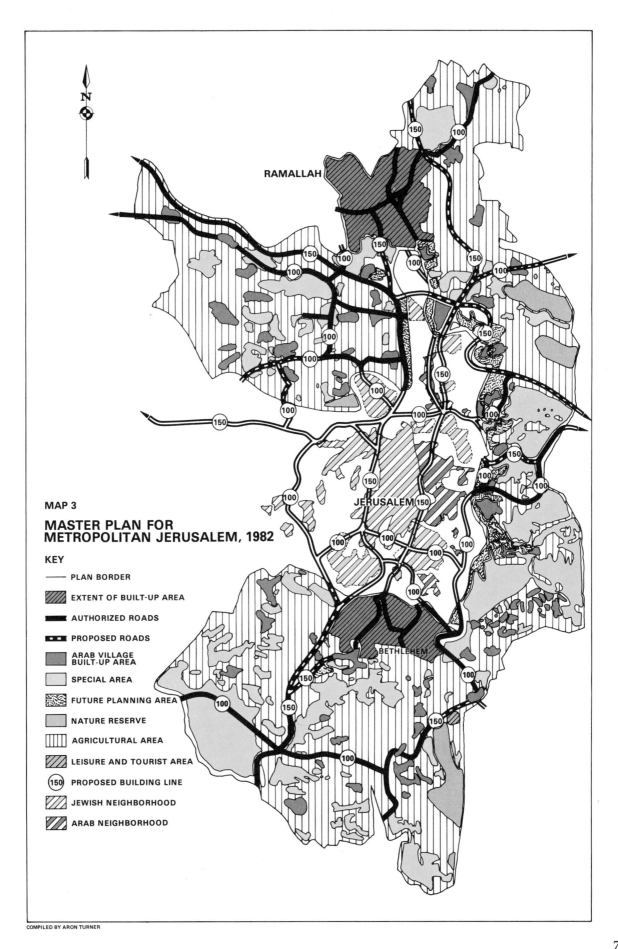

N

MAP 3

**MASTER PLAN FOR
METROPOLITAN JERUSALEM, 1982**

KEY

———— PLAN BORDER

EXTENT OF BUILT-UP AREA

AUTHORIZED ROADS

PROPOSED ROADS

ARAB VILLAGE
BUILT-UP AREA

SPECIAL AREA

FUTURE PLANNING AREA

NATURE RESERVE

AGRICULTURAL AREA

LEISURE AND TOURIST AREA

150 PROPOSED BUILDING LINE

JEWISH NEIGHBORHOOD

ARAB NEIGHBORHOOD

RAMALLAH

JERUSALEM

BETHLEHEM

COMPILED BY ARON TURNER

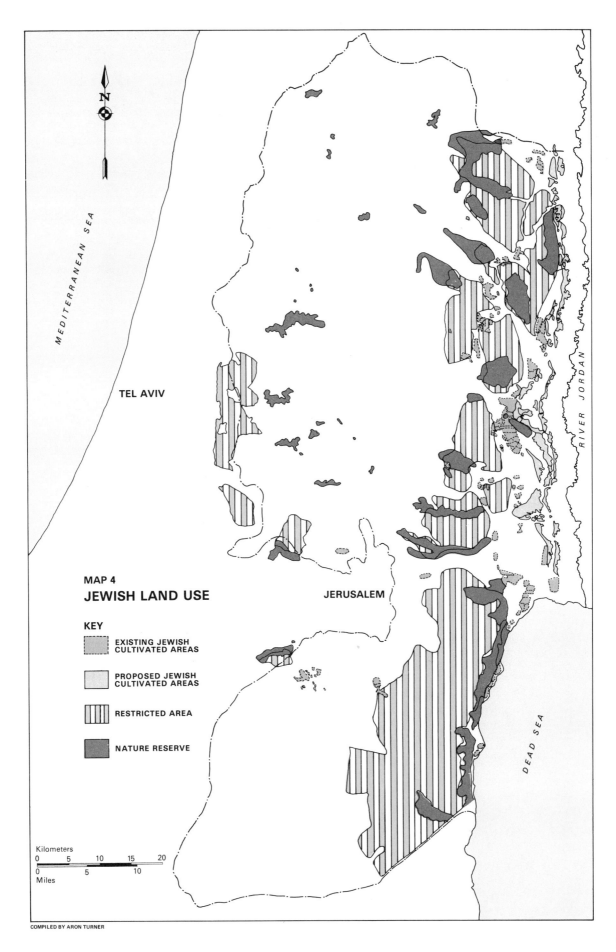

N

MEDITERRANEAN SEA

TEL AVIV

RIVER JORDAN

JERUSALEM

DEAD SEA

MAP 4
JEWISH LAND USE

KEY

EXISTING JEWISH
CULTIVATED AREAS

PROPOSED JEWISH
CULTIVATED AREAS

RESTRICTED AREA

NATURE RESERVE

Kilometers
0   5   10   15   20

0   5   10
Miles

COMPILED BY ARON TURNER

79

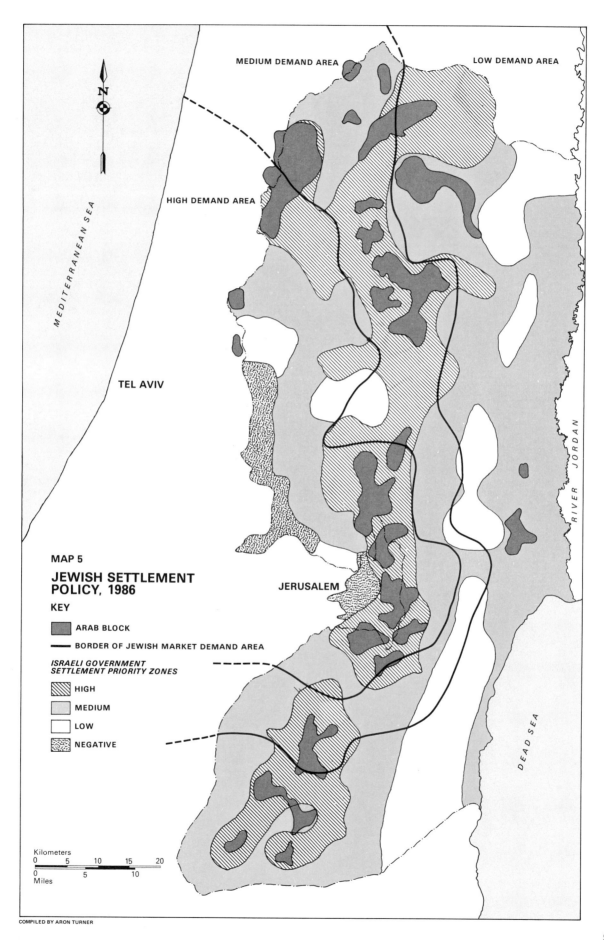

MEDIUM DEMAND AREA

LOW DEMAND AREA

HIGH DEMAND AREA

MEDITERRANEAN SEA

TEL AVIV

RIVER JORDAN

MAP 5

JEWISH SETTLEMENT POLICY, 1986

KEY

ARAB BLOCK

BORDER OF JEWISH MARKET DEMAND AREA

ISRAELI GOVERNMENT SETTLEMENT PRIORITY ZONES

HIGH

MEDIUM

LOW

NEGATIVE

JERUSALEM

DEAD SEA

Kilometers
0   5   10   15   20
0   5   10
Miles

COMPILED BY ARON TURNER

81

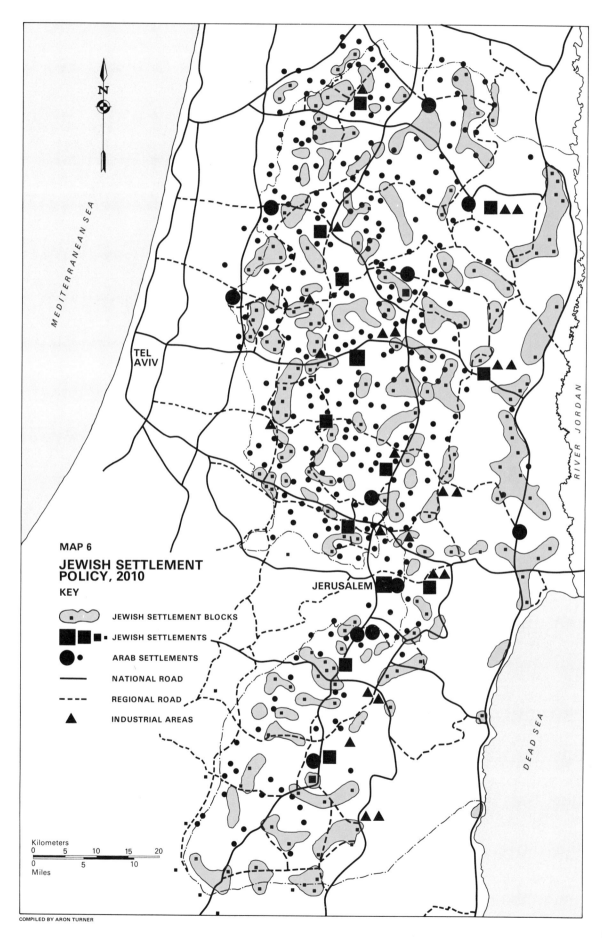

MEDITERRANEAN SEA

TEL
AVIV

JERUSALEM

RIVER JORDAN

DEAD SEA

N

MAP 6

**JEWISH SETTLEMENT
POLICY, 2010**

KEY

⬛🟦▪ JEWISH SETTLEMENTS

JEWISH SETTLEMENT BLOCKS

⬤● ARAB SETTLEMENTS

—— NATIONAL ROAD

---- REGIONAL ROAD

▲ INDUSTRIAL AREAS

Kilometers
0   5   10   15   20

0   5   10
Miles

COMPILED BY ARON TURNER

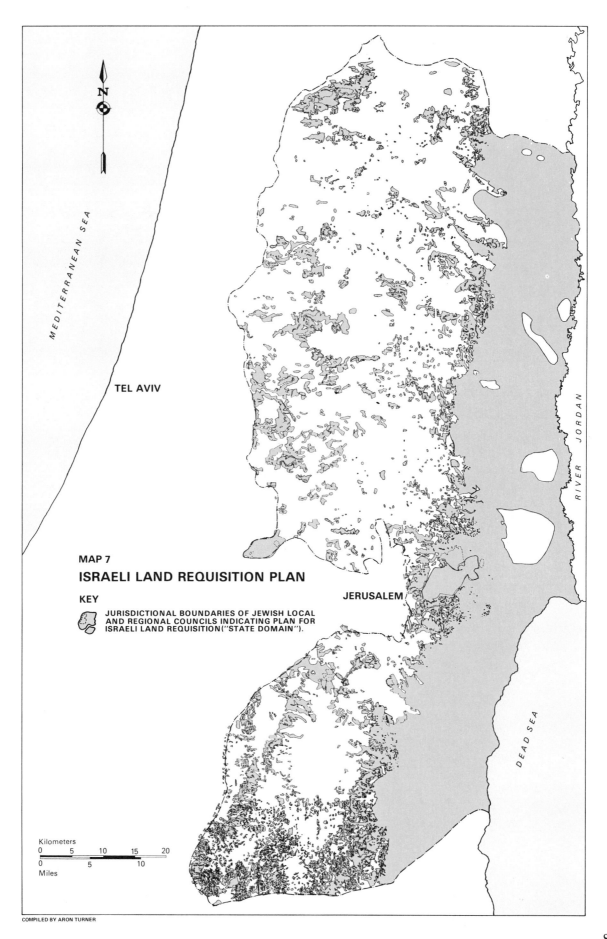

MEDITERRANEAN SEA

N

TEL AVIV

RIVER JORDAN

MAP 7

ISRAELI LAND REQUISITION PLAN

KEY

JURISDICTIONAL BOUNDARIES OF JEWISH LOCAL
AND REGIONAL COUNCILS INDICATING PLAN FOR
ISRAELI LAND REQUISITION ("STATE DOMAIN").

JERUSALEM

DEAD SEA

Kilometers
0   5   10   15   20
0   5   10
Miles

COMPILED BY ARON TURNER

85

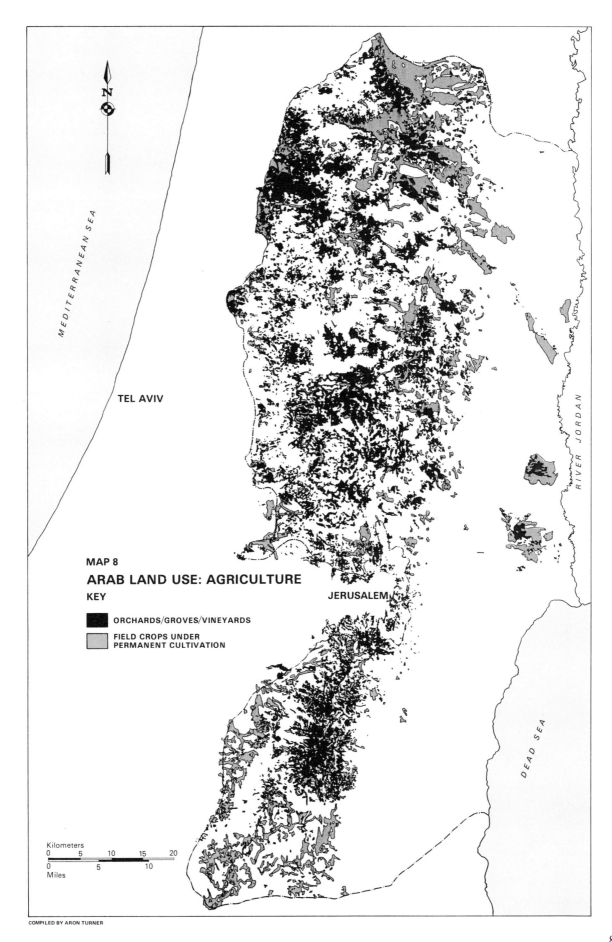

N

MEDITERRANEAN SEA

TEL AVIV

RIVER JORDAN

MAP 8

ARAB LAND USE: AGRICULTURE

KEY

■ ORCHARDS/GROVES/VINEYARDS

▨ FIELD CROPS UNDER
PERMANENT CULTIVATION

JERUSALEM

DEAD SEA

Kilometers
0   5   10   15   20

0   5   10
Miles

COMPILED BY ARON TURNER

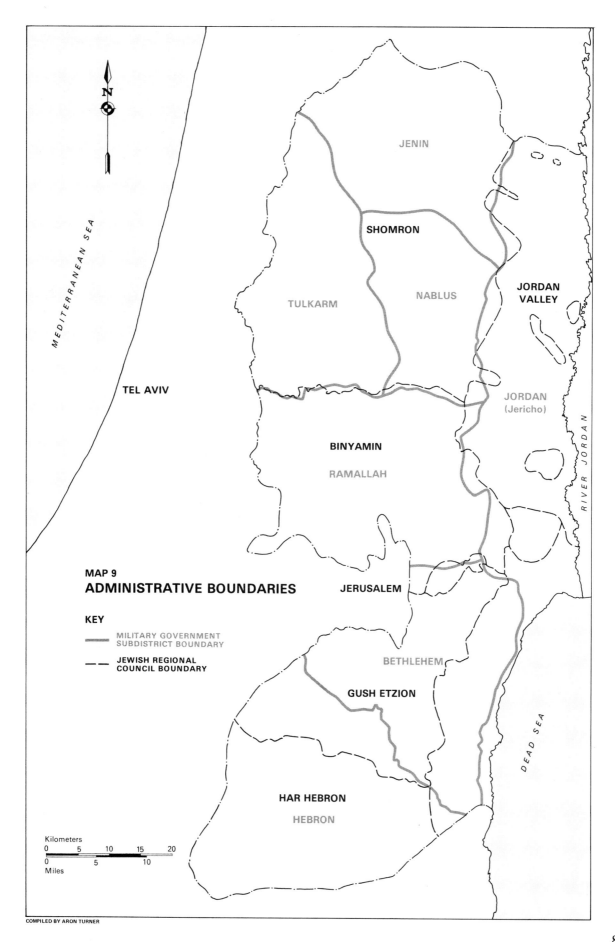

MAP 9
ADMINISTRATIVE BOUNDARIES

KEY

MILITARY GOVERNMENT
SUBDISTRICT BOUNDARY

JEWISH REGIONAL
COUNCIL BOUNDARY

MEDITERRANEAN SEA

N

JENIN

SHOMRON

TULKARM

NABLUS

JORDAN
VALLEY

TEL AVIV

JORDAN
(Jericho)

RIVER JORDAN

BINYAMIN

RAMALLAH

JERUSALEM

BETHLEHEM

GUSH ETZION

DEAD SEA

HAR HEBRON

HEBRON

Kilometers
0   5   10   15   20
0   5   10
Miles

COMPILED BY ARON TURNER

89

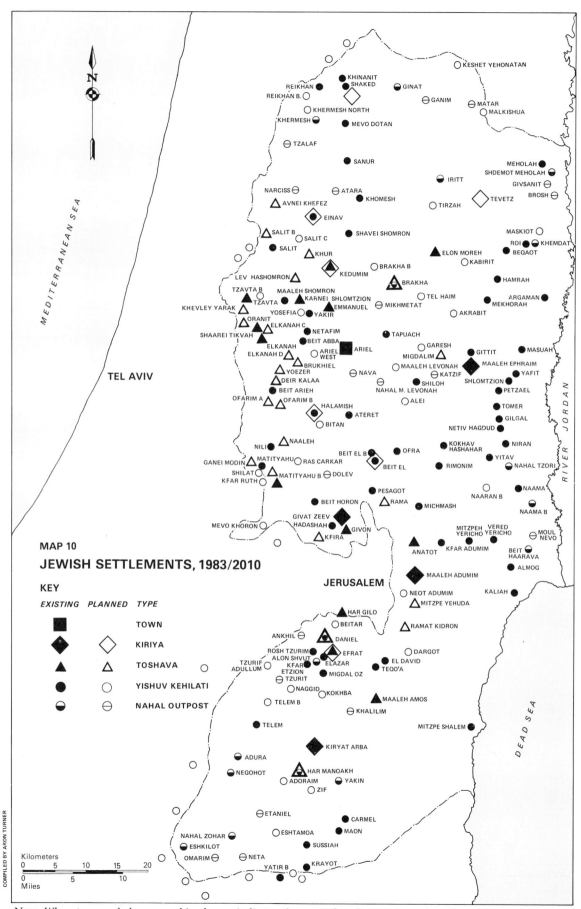

MAP 10
JEWISH SETTLEMENTS, 1983/2010

KEY

EXISTING	PLANNED	TYPE
■	□	**TOWN**
◆	◇	**KIRIYA**
▲	△	**TOSHAVA**
●	○	**YISHUV KEHILATI**
◐	◒	**NAHAL OUTPOST**

MEDITERRANEAN SEA

TEL AVIV

JERUSALEM

RIVER JORDAN

DEAD SEA

COMPILED BY ARON TURNER

Kilometers
0   5   10   15   20

Miles
0   5   10

KESHET YEHONATAN
KHINANIT
SHAKED
REIKHAN
REIKHAN B.
GINAT
GANIM
MATAR
MALKISHUA
KHERMESH NORTH
KHERMESH
MEVO DOTAN
TZALAF
SANUR
MEHOLAH
SHDEMOT MEHOLAH
GIVSANIT
IRITT
BROSH
NARCISS
ATARA
KHOMESH
TIRZAH
MASKIOT
ROI KHEMDAT
AVNEI KHEFEZ
EINAV
BEQAOT
SALIT B
SALIT C
SHAVEI SHOMRON
ELON MOREH
SALIT
KHUR
KABIRIT
HAMRAH
LEV HASHOMRON
KEDUMIM
BRAKHA B
BRAKHA
TZAVTA B
MAALEH SHOMRON
KARNEI SHLOMTZION
TEL HAIM
ARGAMAN
KHEVLEY YARAK
TZAVTA
EMMANUEL
MIKHMETAT
MEKHORAH
YOSEFIA
YAKIR
AKRABIT
ORANIT
ELKANAH C
NETAFIM
SHAAREI TIKVAH
BEIT ABBA
TAPUACH
ELKANAH
ARIEL
GARESH
MASUAH
ELKANAH D
MIGDALIM
GITTIT
ARIEL WEST
MAALEH LEVONAH
MAALEH EPHRAIM
BRUKHIEL
NAVA
KATZIF
YAFIT
YOEZER
SHILOH
SHLOMTZION
DEIR KALAA
NAHAL M. LEVONAH
PETZAEL
BEIT ARIEH
OFARIM A
OFARIM B
ALEI
TOMER
HALAMISH
GILGAL
ATERET
BITAN
NETIV HAGDUD
NAALEH
KOKHAV HASHAHAR
NIRAN
NILI
OFRA
GANEI MODIN
MATITYAHU
RAS CARKAR
BEIT EL B
YITAV
SHILAT
DOLEV
BEIT EL
RIMONIM
NAHAL TZORI
KFAR RUTH
MATITYAHU B
NAAMA
PESAGOT
NAARAN B
BEIT HORON
RAMA
MICHMASH
NAAMA B
MEVO KHORON
GIVAT ZEEV
HADASHAH
KFIRA
GIVON
MITZPEH YERICHO
VERED YERICHO
MOUL NEVO
ANATOT
KFAR ADUMIM
BEIT HAARAVA
MAALEH ADUMIM
ALMOG
NEOT ADUMIM
KALIAH
MITZPE YEHUDA
HAR GILO
BEITAR
RAMAT KIDRON
ANKHIL
DANIEL
ROSH TZURIM
EFRAT
DARGOT
ALON SHVUT
ELAZAR
EL DAVID
TZURIF ADULLUM
KFAR ETZION
MIGDAL OZ
TEQO'A
TZURIT
NAGGID
KOKHBA
TELEM B
MAALEH AMOS
TELEM
KHALILIM
MITZPE SHALEM
KIRYAT ARBA
ADURA
NEGOHOT
HAR MANOAKH
ADORAIM
YAKIN
ZIF
ETANIEL
CARMEL
NAHAL ZOHAR
ESHTAMOA
MAON
ESHKILOT
SUSSIAH
OMARIM
NETA
YATIR B
KRAYOT

NOTE: When two symbols are combined, one indicates the type of settlement that exists, the other the type that is planned. For example, the symbol ◭ denotes an existing yishuv kehilati and a planned toshava.

91

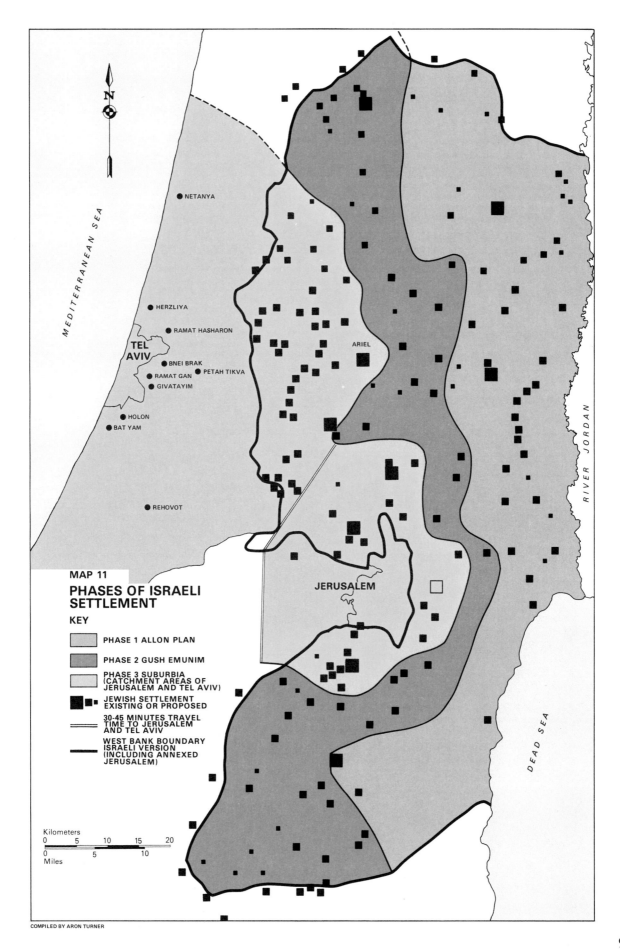

N

MEDITERRANEAN SEA

● NETANYA

● HERZLIYA

● RAMAT HASHARON

TEL AVIV

● BNEI BRAK
● PETAH TIKVA
● RAMAT GAN
● GIVATAYIM

● HOLON
● BAT YAM

● REHOVOT

ARIEL

JERUSALEM

RIVER JORDAN

DEAD SEA

MAP 11

PHASES OF ISRAELI SETTLEMENT

KEY

PHASE 1 ALLON PLAN

PHASE 2 GUSH EMUNIM

PHASE 3 SUBURBIA (CATCHMENT AREAS OF JERUSALEM AND TEL AVIV)

■ ■ JEWISH SETTLEMENT EXISTING OR PROPOSED

30-45 MINUTES TRAVEL TIME TO JERUSALEM AND TEL AVIV

WEST BANK BOUNDARY ISRAELI VERSION (INCLUDING ANNEXED JERUSALEM)

Kilometers
0   5   10   15   20
0   5   10
Miles

COMPILED BY ARON TURNER

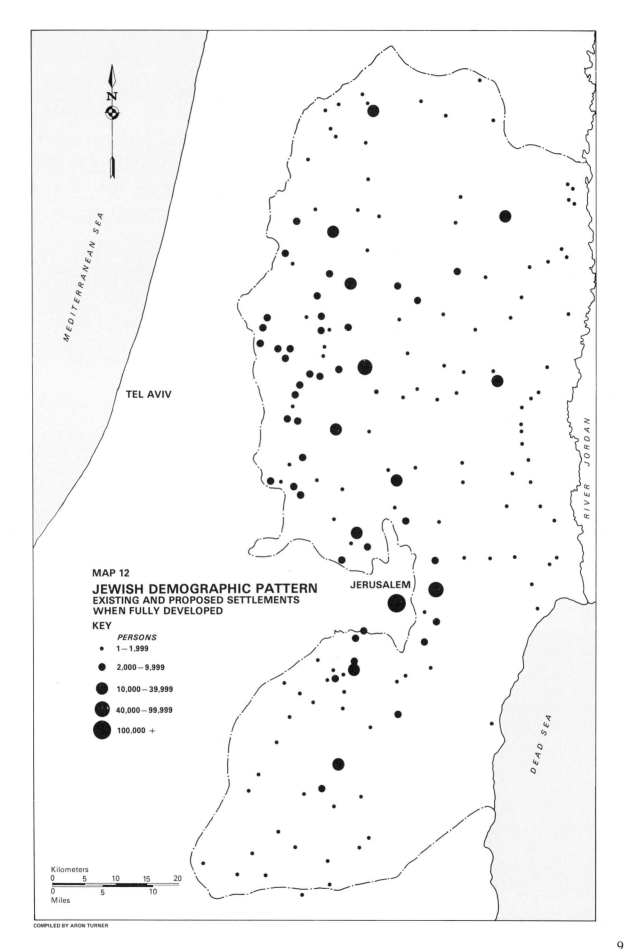

MAP 12

JEWISH DEMOGRAPHIC PATTERN
EXISTING AND PROPOSED SETTLEMENTS
WHEN FULLY DEVELOPED

KEY

PERSONS

·   1 — 1,999

●   2,000 — 9,999

●   10,000 — 39,999

●   40,000 — 99,999

●   100,000 +

MEDITERRANEAN SEA

TEL AVIV

JERUSALEM

RIVER JORDAN

DEAD SEA

Kilometers
0   5   10   15   20
0   5   10
Miles

COMPILED BY ARON TURNER

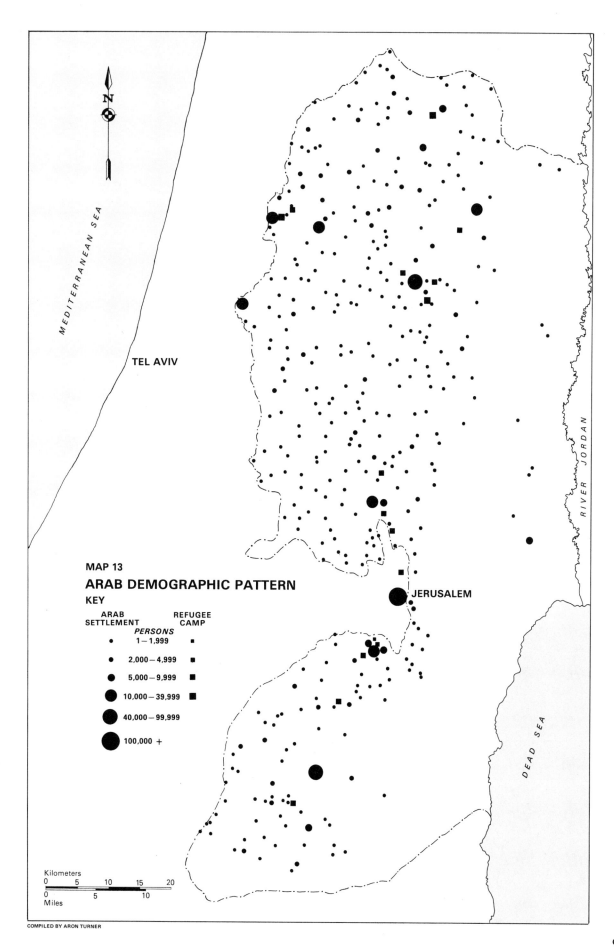

MAP 13

ARAB DEMOGRAPHIC PATTERN

KEY

ARAB SETTLEMENT		REFUGEE CAMP
PERSONS		
•	1 — 1,999	▪
•	2,000 — 4,999	▪
●	5,000 — 9,999	■
●	10,000 — 39,999	■
●	40,000 — 99,999	
●	100,000 +	

MEDITERRANEAN SEA

TEL AVIV

RIVER JORDAN

JERUSALEM

DEAD SEA

Kilometers
0   5   10   15   20
0   5   10
Miles

COMPILED BY ARON TURNER

97

A Note on the Book

This book was edited by Marcia Brubeck
and by Donna Spitler of the
Publications Staff of the American Enterprise Institute.
The staff also designed the cover and format, with Pat Taylor.
The maps were drawn by Hördur Karlsson and Carlos Cornelio.
The typeface used for the text of this book is
Palatino, designed by Hermann Zapf.
The type was set by
Hendricks-Miller Typographic Company, of Washington, D.C.
Thomson-Shore, Inc., of Dexter, Michigan,
printed and bound the book, using Warren's Olde Style paper.